Crackers & Peaches
Travels in Georgia

Published by Milner Press, Atlanta Georgia.

Manufactured in the United States of America.

International Standard Book Number 0-9626112-1-2

First Printing

5   4   3   2   1

Book and cover designed by Steve Roumas using a Macintosh LCIII. The text is set in 11/13 Times Roman.

Maps compiled by Steve Roumas

Illustrations by Susan Evans Harper

Printed by United Book Press, Inc., Baltimore, Maryland, 21207

Library of Congress Cataloging-in-Publication Data:

Schnell, Jane. 1930-
      Crackers & Peaches : Travels in Georgia / by Jane Schnell.
          p.   cm.
      Includes Index.
      ISBN 0-9626112-1-2 : $11.00
      1. Georgia--Description and travel.   2. Bicycle touring--Georgia
I. Title.   II. Title: Crackers and Peaches
f291.2.S36 1993   93-8249
917.5804'43--dc20   CIP

Other Books by Jane Schnell

Changing Gears:
Bicycling America's Perimeter

Milner Press 1990

Tibetan Rug News
1984

About the Illustrator

Although Susan Evans Harper never misses an oppertunity to do illustrations, her preferred medium is watercolor. she studied at the Slade School of Fine Artsin London but now lives in the United States. Her work has been seen in one-woman shows in her native England and in group shows in Washington D.C. A set of her watercolors hangs in the Smithsonian castle. Her favorite subject are industrial and urban landscapes, church interiors, and American trucks. (See index for list of illustrations.)

Crackers & Peaches

Travels in Georgia

Jane Schnell

To Nancy with best wishes from Jane Schnell

Milner Press
Atlanta, Georgia
1993

Contents

Dedicated to Mom,
Ruth McCullough Schnell

First, I thank my parents for my birth in Georgia and a happy childhood there. Second, I thank the people of Georgia for a splendid tour and the bicyclists whose hours of voluntary efforts have created events I've enjoyed. Third, I thank the long list of people who helped *Crackers & Peaches* become a book. I confine the list to major contributors, in addition to people who populate the story. Since I neither spell nor punctuate and don't do verbs, these matters, and others, were tended to by Jane D. Knight, Earl Johnson and, Michelle Paul. Without the constructive criticism of Emily Wright, Senior Editor, Peachtree Publications, Inc., I would not have known how to revise the book or focus the editing of Barbara Miller and Dr. Martha B. Binford. In addition, these editors kept me as close to the book's subject as they could. Voluntary readers Janis L. Knorr, Frank T. Schnell, Charles T. Hill, Carolyn Hodges, Ruth M. Schnell, Dorothy S. Chesnut, Whitney Painter, and many others, including those who provided comments on the back cover, swept up my mistakes, usually faster than I made them. Now that the book is printed, I would appreciate readers who find confusions or inaccuracies letting me know so that they will not be repeated in future editions.

Special thanks to Dr. Kathryn S. Hawes, Coordinator, Reading/Study Skills, Memphis State University Developmental Studies, for writing the Lesson Plans and to Georgie Meuth Mundell for editing them. I included the Lesson Plans because I never liked textbooks. My hope is that some Georgia students will enjoy reading *Crackers & Peaches* for an outsider's view of places they know well. Then, perhaps, it would be fun for them as well as instructive to find things I didn't or expand upon what I noticed. I can't imagine what it would be to live without reading, so I hope there will be newly literate people who will find these Travels in Georgia worth the effort.

Once we got the text under control artists Susan Evans Harper illustrated it and Stephen Roumas designed the book and cover.

Thanks to the Georgia Department of Industry, Trade, and Tourism for the maps and to Barbara Daniel and Karin Pendley Koser for their assistance.

There were many other contributions to me and to the book by supportive, cheering friends. The biggest thanks goes to my mother, who cheers loudest of all. Thank you all.

Forward

Jane Schnell's *Crackers & Peaches* covers the state of Georgia in a variety of ways. In constructing her narrative she rides around the entire state on her bicycle, and on her way introduces us to a variety of interesting and diverse people, who, she assures us, like to talk. On another level, Schnell also takes us on a tour of the state's natural history and the interactions between the natural environment and the people who have moved through it. So we are introduced to ancient Cherokee pathways and to contemporary museums which recapture some of Georgia's rich and diverse heritage. Always interesting *Crackers & Peaches,* is more than a travelogue, more than an account of interesting people, it is a true guide to all that the name Georgia implies. At one point we find her on the same route as the famous naturalist, William Bartram: at another we are in Augusta learning some of the lore associated with the world's most famous golf tournament. Later we join her in watching a fine film about "the Chatthoochee Legacy" in Columbus. Then again we find her enjoying an out-of-the way cafe and adding another entry to her list of creatively-named beauty salons. Anyone who prefers to poke about back roads and thereby discover the real Georgia will find *Crackers & Peaches* absorbing, informative and consistently entertaining.

—Joseph M. Hawes,
Professor of History, Memphis State University

Jane Schnell's path around the perimeter of Georgia

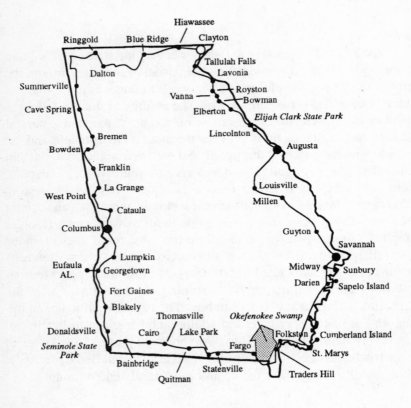

Introduction

Fifty years after my first departure, I decided to pedal the perimeter of the state of Georgia, alone, and see what would happen. I returned to my native state with my bicycle, wondering what adventure lay beyond my front wheel.

I'm a Georgian and a Southerner by birth; a big-city, Mid-Atlantic civil servant by profession. Between my youth in Georgia and college in Virginia, I was a military dependent, living with my parents in Berlin and attending school in Switzerland. My first job after college was for the U.S. Army in what was then West Germany. Then, for over thirty years, I wore a head-set, sifting international information in Washington, D.C., for the Central Intelligence Agency. Vacations were spent abroad, hiking or skiing. For recreation, I managed real estate, made enameled jewelry, and imported rugs in small quantities for sale.

But in my heart, I remained Georgian enough to feel insulted when people in Atlanta joked that I was a "Fed" who sounded like a Yankee. I disliked hearing criticism from the people I was working to protect, while at the same time, I appreciated the spotlight their comments threw on my isolation from our country and my ignorance of my own roots.

So, as a retirement present, I gave myself a bicycle tour of the country I'd worked so long and hard for but had hardly seen (chronicled in my book *Changing Gears*). During that tour, Courtney Gaines of Savannah persuaded me to pedal the BRAG, Bicycle Ride Across Georgia. On BRAG's first day, as I was standing among strangers, someone asked, "Where is everyone from? I'm from Macon." The replies came: Atlanta, Gwinnett, Rome, Cairo, and many other Georgia locations. When it was my turn, I said, "Columbus." The whole group exploded,

"You sure don't sound like you're from Columbus!"

"You don't act like anyone from Columbus!"

"You don't even think like a Columbus person!"

"Why do you claim to be from Columbus?"

Wondering how they knew what I thought, I replied, "Because I was born there." A moment of stunned silence gave way to laughter and chatter, including one person who said, "I thought you meant Ohio."

In shock, I smiled, the moment passed, and I felt accepted. But they were right. Though I had spent the past 50 years of my life somewhere else — Ohio, Europe, Nepal, Singapore, and Washington, D.C. — it had never occurred to me that I was other than a Georgian, from Muscogee County, Columbus, Georgia, USA. Hadn't I, for my first eleven years, felt Georgia red clay between my toes and scuppernongs between my teeth? Didn't I still work to speak faster so people wouldn't go away before the sentence ended?

Well, I learned something every day of the BRAG, three years in a row. I certainly learned that I wanted to see more of Georgia than I could see in one week a year of pedaling with hundreds of others who become a temporary mobile village. A solo bicycle tour of Georgia's perimeter seemed the perfect way to do just that. This book expands my letters from the road (dubbed "pedalgrams" by one recipient) during that six-week tour in 1991. Written as a journal, *Crackers & Peaches* takes you, vicariously, on my bicycle and into Georgia, beyond the metropolitan heart of Atlanta, into the body of the state; it shares the joys of vagabond rambling. My hope is that it will make more friends for myself and for the state of Georgia and that you will enjoy rambling with me. I hope, too, that it will encourage you to read, travel, and wander further, following your own dreams.

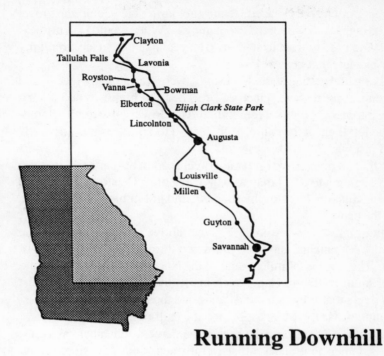

Running Downhill

Possum Trot Cabin, Rabun County, Georgia, Wednesday, March 6

At my cabin in the north Georgia mountains, I gazed out the window and shivered. Departure day had dawned forbiddingly cold, overcast, and sunless. Hunching back under the covers, I lamented that I'd told anyone about my intended pilgrimage around my home state of Georgia. "Me and my big mouth," I thought miserably. Although I'd planned and trained for this trip, it would have been nice to start with some sunshine.

Reluctantly, I dragged myself out of my warm bed and showered. The weather did not improve. The gray day still did not beckon me to start an out-of-doors journey, but I went about my preparations, turning off the water to the house, loading my bicycle. "No point in stalling," I thought. "I decided to do this two-month, self-contained bicycle camping tour, so I'd better just do it!"

Pushing my heavily loaded Centurion touring bicycle up the gravel road to the highway, I wondered about things. "When would I get my next shower? Did I really want to start my 61st year like this? Gee, aren't my sleeping bag and tent heavy?"

Walking and getting started, however, were warming my feet — and strengthening my resolve. Just as I reached the highway and started thinking happier thoughts, I remembered my lower false teeth! Somehow I had left them at the cabin. "Oh dear," I thought, "is this an omen? Should I just wait?"

Just then, a man drove onto the gravel road in his car and I flagged him. "If I can get a ride, I may as well carry on." He slowed. I leaned the bike against the bank of the road cut and got in his car for the ride back to the cabin.

At the highway, we were 2,200 feet above sea level, among the Blue Ridge Mountains, and three miles uphill from the Georgia town of Clayton. The town is 20 miles south of the North Carolina state line and 10 miles south of Rabun Gap, which marks the watershed between the Georgia rivers that flow into the Atlantic and the Little Tennessee River, which empties, via the Mississippi, into the Gulf of Mexico.

The whole Clayton area is a resort wilderness inhabited by locals, tourists, summer Floridians, artists, craftsmen, and, occasionally, by people like me. Possum Trot itself is a community of one-acre lots, some with all-weather small houses. It is a place for individualists.

During the short, bumping descent to Possum Trot, the driver introduced himself as Dan O'Keith. He lived in Clayton several months at a time. Originally from New England, he and his wife had come up from Florida, liked it, and kept returning.

I got out at the fork in the road and thanked him. I had already met the first new person on my journey! I walked up to my house, put my teeth in, and briskly hiked back to my bike, lighter hearted and more confident.

When doubt creeps up on me, I try to remember that it isn't what happens that's important in life, it's what I make of it. Anyone can look back, but challenge lies ahead.

I got on the bike and finally pedaled my first stroke. I was on my way!

When I rolled into Clayton, however, I stopped again and leaned my bike against a storefront. During the ride, I noticed that the bag of last-minute items, including a few books and papers, was too heavy on top of the heap. It's amazing what you can feel on a loaded bicycle, and I could tell that my load was not balanced. I put the bag under the tent and put the lighter sleeping bag on top.

I smiled as many people waved when they saw me working on the loaded bicycle. A bicycle traveler always seems to draw attention.

As I rearranged the tie-down bungee cords, I told myself to quit stalling and get going. I pedaled up to the stoplight on Main Street. When the light turned to green, I made the decision to ride on Old 441 (Main Street) instead of the shoulder of US 441 South.

Old 441 led me out of town and down the mountain, past a "Rain-Free Hay" sign, and through Tiger. Mist grew heavy and turned to rain. I huddled down into my raingear, feeling the sweat inside meet and mingle with the rain from outside. I kept on, mainly because I was riding along a training route I knew well. Familiarity with an area breeds confidence on a bike.

Wiley and Lakemont were the next towns, each consisting of only a few buildings, a post office, and perhaps one store. Many people lived here only in the summer or on weekends. Referred to as "lake people" by the full-time residents, they had places on the mountain overlooking Lake Rabun or along its shore. Locals lived in the small towns or on valley bottom farms, though some also lived around the lakes.

At Lakemont, the road turned sharply left, crossed the Tallulah River, then ran parallel to it. The gentle rain had stopped. Birds began to sing and dogs barked, not in anger but to announce my passing as I continued to roll downhill beside the Tallulah River. I would have called it a creek had I not learned its name.

As I rode, I recalled my first long swim across Lake Rabun and happy visits to the Chesnut family home as I was growing up in the 1930s. World War II took our family away from Georgia when I was eleven, but my mother's friends had drawn us back to visit. These experiences and memories led me to build the little house at Possum Trot to retire in. It was designed by Norwood Griffin and built by his son, Lakemont's Volunteer Fire Chief, Bill Griffin. There I left my car and began my journey.

Instead of riding over the dam at Tallulah Falls, I stopped again and went inside to see the Georgia Power exhibit at Terrora. A series of dams, built about 1916, created more electricity for Georgia, but they had also left Tallulah Falls a whisper of its former self. The central attraction of northeast Georgia's resorts was cut to a trickle and fell silent in the 1920s. Sightseers, honeymooners, families, and vacationers had once come by private railroad, wagon, even on foot in Victorian times — as had the Indians earlier — to view the cascades of the Tallulah River thundering through the oldest natural gorge in the United States.

Second in depth to the Grand Canyon, the now-wooded Tallulah Gorge is 1,100 feet deep and, unlike Niagara Falls, is only a narrow 820 feet across. The great circus performer, Walenda, walked a wire across the Tallulah Falls gorge. I stood near the spot where this spectacle had taken place and imagined how formidable the falls must have been when the Indians lived here. Sighing, I took up the heavy bicycle again, leaving the beautiful silence in my wake.

As I pedaled down, and most ruefully up, I thought about my packing abilities. After as much cycle touring as I've done, I should be an expert. Still, I had managed to bring a few "luxuries" on this trip — some I was already regretting. I'd brought three rain jackets (when one would be enough), three or four T-shirts, even a spare pair of shoes, and a change into "real" clothes, in this case a silk pant suit that supposedly weighed almost nothing. Since completing the self-contained bicycle tour chronicled in *Changing Gears,* I had only toured with a "sag" vehicle to carry clothes and equipment. Obviously, I had lost the knack for traveling light.

As more proof of that loss, I have to admit I'd added a new, 6.5 pound Compaq notebook computer! Concealed among the panniers and gear were the computer, wires to plug it in, an abbreviated instruction manual, and disks with mailers for letters to my friends, as well as backup writing pads and pens, two cameras, and a dozen rolls of film! As before, I carried a small dictation machine for telling my story. I planned to transcribe the tapes daily or when there was time.

The list of "necessities" for this trip also included favorite snacks such as a dozen Meal-to-Go bars, PowerBars, Turkish apricots, my "tonic," a mix of 14 herbs with potassium called KM, and Nutri/System Craving Control Snacks. I'd recently lost 25 pounds and had no desire to eat them back. Experience has taught me that at 50 miles a day I gain weight instead of losing it because one of the major entertainments on the road alone is sitting in a home or family restaurant, talking with the people and sampling the fare.

Not only was my Centurion bicycle too heavy for this trip, but I could not stand on the pedals going up hills. If I did the precarious balance caused the bike to fishtail. I was going to have to climb sitting down. Racers have told me that sitting while climbing is a sign of strength. "I'll continue to believe that!" I thought.

I planned my route around Georgia's perimeter on state and AAA maps and guides. My intent was to roll downhill to Savannah, where, after the first week, it would be warmer. I could leave heavier clothing, I would have eaten much of the snack food, and — hooray! — the bicycle would be much lighter. Anyhow, along the flat seacoastal terrain, weight wouldn't be so critical unless there was a severe headwind.

My route would take me south from Savannah to St. Marys and then west toward Thomasville and the Alabama line. From there, I would start north. Upon reaching Columbus, where I was born, I would spend a week on a local farm, resting and helping with spring planting. Then, stronger and with a lighter bicycle, returning to the mountains of north Georgia shouldn't pose a huge obstacle.

That was the plan, but you can't plan for reality. I knew the trip would take on a life of its own, inserting humps and bumps and letting joy unroll, making a path for my wheels. I just never knew what a day would hand me in weather, encounters, hills, museums, or just plain happy pedaling.

Although my Centurion bike was overloaded, I was delighted that the 300 miles a month I had ridden in January and February had put my legs on notice.

Watching a hawk fly away, I cranked along, passing up the temptation to enter Magnolia Antique Store at Turnerville. I took a "long cut" that avoided traffic and wound up in Hollywood on the highway I'd left. A few hundred yards more brought me to the junction with GA Route 17. This road carried me up and down over hill and creek, forced me to walk a short steep bit, then sent me flying downhill on wind-singing wheels, and up again into Toccoa, to an altitude of about 1,000 feet.

Going through town, I added "The HeadQuarters" to my unwritten list of amusing beauty shop names. I read the time and temperature — 12:42 P.M., 50 degrees — on the bank sign, glanced up a "Thank you" for the lack of precipitation and the filtered sun, and stopped at Wendy's for a baked potato with broccoli (no cheese), washed down with decaffeinated coffee.

In an even better mood, I took to the road again. There is never enough time to see and do everything. I must choose or come back. The nature of life is selection. When I choose well, progress occurs with fewer bumps. Poor choices allow experience to indicate a need for change. These subtleties require attention, for they are the journey's map.

Thus, the time of day, the hills, and a "Closed" notice deterred me from a detour to see Traveler's Rest, a plantation, inn, and stagecoach stop in the 1830s. I would have to come back. Every decision is both for and against something. I knew that something would replace Traveler's Rest. I just didn't know what — yet.

Reading historical markers from a bicycle requires no slamming on of car brakes, no turning, no backing up. I'd been pedaling along a ridge for some time when I came to the town of Martin. It looked vaguely familiar. I slowed, bounced over the railroad tracks, and halted by a historical marker under the water tank. Then I remembered that I had stopped here during the annual Bicycle Ride Across Georgia (BRAG) a few years back. Because I did not remember the story the marker told, I reread it:

> **Red Hollow Road:** Winding along a ridge from the mouth of Broad River to the head of Tugalo, Red Hollow Road evolved from upper Cherokee Path and became a complex pioneer road system. In 1736 to 1737 James Oglethorpe, who founded Georgia in 1733, had River Road laid out from Augusta to Savannah. It was Georgia's first long road built by white men. At Augusta, River Road joined upper Cherokee Path whose origins are lost in antiquity. From Augusta northward to Petersburg, the Path became Petersburg Road. The Path crossed not a single stream for approximately 70 miles between Petersburg and Toccoa. Continuing north to a point near Martin, the Path became Red Hollow Road. The Road junctioned at Toccoa with Unicoi Turnpike, which ran into east Tennessee. The Road at Toccoa also had a spur, Locust Stake Road, which ran to the GA/NC line. The tracks of the Southern RR, completed in 1878, cut Red Hollow Road thirteen times between Toccoa and Martin.

From Hollywood to Martin, I'd been riding on GA 17, a modern, slightly straightened Red Hollow Road. I looked up at a shiny water tower which resembled a huge flying saucer, then continued along the historic ridge route. By midafternoon, it was quite gray, and almost, but not quite, drizzling. At a McDonald's on the edge of Lavonia, I bought a cup of hot coffee and promptly spilled it. The 48 miles I'd pedaled had caught up with me. I sat and studied the map while I sipped from the refilled cup.

I had not locked my bicycle because it was on the other side of the window. Occasionally, I looked up and checked on it. I saw a man with a religious collar walk up and study the bike. Finishing my coffee, I gathered my things and went outside. The Reverend Dexter Moser, retired pastor of the Evangelical Lutheran Church of America, asked where I was going and where I had come from. He told me of friends and acquaintances of his who cycled, and wished me well on the journey.

I pushed the heavy bicycle through McDonald's parking lot, rode it across GA 17, and got off. The rear tire was flat! So much for my hopes of a flat-free tour! I was standing in front of a Days Inn and thought about registering for the night.

"No," I admonished myself, "There is no reason to carry all this camping equipment if you are going to duck into a motel every night. There is plenty of time to reach Hart State Park. You can't begin a tour by crumbling at the first difficulty. Just sit down and fix the tire; you know it won't take long."

Thus self-instructed, I looked around for cover while I fixed the tire. I eyed the entrance to the Days Inn and decided the management might not like my decorating it with bags, bicycle tires, and bits and pieces of clothing and equipment. I pushed on to a grassy spot between the Days Inn and a motorcycle store.

Although I was a bit out of practice, I knew it shouldn't take more than minutes to fix the tire. Hart State Park, where I planned to camp, probably wasn't more than an hour or two away so I took my time and patched the tube instead of hunting around in the panniers for the new tubes, mainly because I couldn't remember where I'd put them.

An East Indian man came up. "I have some tools in my car. Do you need anything?" he asked.

"How kind of you. No, I'm just finishing," I said, picking up the pump to fill the tire with air.

"Well, just let me know. I'll be inside," he replied, then stood watching me pump the tire.

"I was just thinking that maybe I should stay here," I said. "Is it your motel?"

"You want to stay? Yes, please stay. No charge. On the house," he answered.

I couldn't believe my ears! "Really?" I gasped.

He nodded and told me he'd be delighted. I should come to the desk when I was ready to get a room key. Because I couldn't move the bicycle without its rear wheel, I continued to pump the tire and reassembled everything while he went on in.

Two men from the motorcycle shop, Centerline Cycles, came to watch and helped hold the bike while I reattached the rear wheel. We talked about how nice most people are to travelers on two wheels (both bicycle and motorcycle). I told them about locking my keys in the car in a filling station and being helped by two Harley-Davison bikers. They were Hells Angels that I'd been watching with apprehension. They were so nice, though, that I'd had to remove a prejudice from my mental database. The men told me they enjoyed my story and wished me luck on my trip.

At the Days Inn desk, Lily Hansen gave me a room key — there was no check-in form — and said she'd lived in Lavonia for 18 years. Her husband was a retired New York City cop, and she had worked for the telephone company at JFK Airport while it was still called Idlewild. She was one of a select group of international phone operators who reported directly to the president of AT&T; the group was his pet project, though someone else came around to supervise them. Lily said she adored the challenge of the work.

Her father owned a trucking company and she also talked about life as a truck driver. She had liked that, too, and had worked at it long enough to pay off some debts. Lily, another woman, and a man drove two trucks — hard — for months, one sleeping while the other two drove in five-hour shifts.

She told me that the insides of the trucks are great, like homes. One fellow she knew spent $180,000 for his truck, took his wife along and drove all over. They had several closets and a king-sized bed in the cab. Everything inside was custom-made.

Lily had been working at the motel for a long time, over a dozen years, and liked that, too. She was a cheery, communicative lady, and I enjoyed listening to her. So often when I stop, people want me to do all the talking about what it's like traveling by bike. Sometimes it's nice to hear someone else's story. One of the things I was beginning to determine about Southerners, in just one day, was that they like to chat.

I wanted to be sure to write a thank-you note to the manager and Lily gave me his card: "Govind N. Patel, General Manager Kamals Enterprises, Inc." When I commented on his unusual generosity, she mentioned that he was a very nice person and she was glad to work for him. He had come to the United States from Bombay to attend college, and had married and raised his family here, returning to India periodically to visit relatives. I got the impression that, unlike their parents, the children, born and brought up here, aren't fond of travel to India.

Finally, I rolled my bike to the room, reflecting on my first day, and called my mom in Smyrna to relate my good fortune. Later, showered and dry, I pushed a button to find out what Oprah was talking about.

Lavonia, Thursday, March 7

A morning person, I usually awaken between five and six. This morning was no exception. It had rained overnight, but appeared to be clearing, as the TV weather channel predicted. I'd been too lazy to go out for supper and had eaten some of the food I carried. I ate several pieces of fruit before having pancakes in the restaurant. I read a newspaper and felt luxurious.

The previous evening (after Oprah), I'd studied the map and decided to stay on GA 17 instead of continuing to Hartwell. I'd been in Hartwell to begin BRAG '90. So, with one eye on the rain clouds and the other on the map, I decided to skip it this time and turned my attention to bike maintenance.

I don't put normal lubricants on my bicycle chain because they make it greasy. Dirt and dust really stick to a greasy chain. Then the grease and dirt come off on my legs and hands and eventually get smeared on my nose, ears, and clothes. Instead, I lubricate the chain of the bicycle by cooking it in hot paraffin, the same material cooks use to cover jelly put up in glasses. Sand, clay, dust, and dirt do not adhere to the paraffin, leaving my bicycle, me, and my equipment cleaner. The drawback is that when the chain gets wet, I have to paraffin it again or it will rust. Sometimes, if it rains in the morning, then gets sunny, and I continue to pedal, the chain dries out and doesn't rust.

In any case, every five hundred miles, or about once a week to ten days on a tour like mine, the chain must be "cooked." I carry a small aluminum bread loaf pan with half an inch of paraffin hardened in the bottom, the smallest back-packing stove I can find, and a can of fuel. The fuel fits in my lowest water bottle cage. (I save the top two cages for water.) The stove fits inside a small pot and leaves enough space for a few matches, a lighter, and the lid. That, a cup, and utensils complete my "kitchen" equipment.

Because it had rained off and on the day before, I inspected the chain, wiped it on a rag, but decided to let it go without cooking it. I had a spare, pre-cooked chain on this trip so I could cook chains when it's convenient. I had not done this before. It was one of the "little extras" that made the bicycle so heavy.

I left the wonderful motel. Ronnie, one of the two motorcyclists, was already in the shop next door. I popped my head into to thank him for his help and ask his opinion on traffic patterns. He agreed that GA 17 would not have much traffic after everyone got where they were going for the day. I waved goodbye and headed for Royston — 12 miles ahead.

This early in March, it was liable to be cold and wet, but as I rolled through Lavonia, it was ten degrees warmer than Possum Trot had been the day before. I was into the undulating Piedmont Plateau now and probably rolling at an average altitude of 700 feet. As I pedaled, the clouds continued to roll away, strengthening the effect of the sun. The grass seemed greener and birds began to sing.

A breeze was blowing and I began to get warm wearing my layers — a long-sleeved wool sweater on top of a short-sleeved wool bicycling jersey, under a lined Gortex rain jacket. I leaned the bike on the Royston city limits sign and removed one of my sweaters and the rain jacket before continuing into Royston, the hometown of baseball player Ty Cobb.

Back in Tallulah Falls, the old railroad station had been made into a craft co-op shop. In Royston, AmeriGas Carbiration uses the old station as a warehouse. I considered collecting new uses for railroad stations and movie theaters as well as names of beauty parlors. In the midst of my reveries, a woman in a jogging suit, wearing radio earphones, shouted across me, and the street, to another jogging-suited woman. "Don't get plumb wore out, now," she warned her friend. I took the caution to heart as well.

Some 20 miles ahead was Elberton. I thought I would reach it in time for lunch. The route was often flat along a ridge or slightly downhill. As on the day before, the further I rolled, the flatter the terrain became.

Several times I saw large flocks of robins migrating.

The next town, Vanna, consisted of a post office and store in one building. The post office door was locked. At the other end of the building, an elderly couple told me the post office had closed two years ago. Its fine granite sign still shone in the sun.

While stopped, I added a bicycle cap with a bill to my helmet attire to cut the sun away from my eyes. New-style helmets are lighter, but few have a visor. I like the one on my old "bucket" helmet.

I worried about the rear tire being soft, but I was too lazy to stop again and pump it up. A tailwind pushed me along GA 17, flat and parallel to the railroad tracks, into Elbert County. Sage brush was blowing away from me.

At the town square in Bowman, I stopped, leaned the bike against a building and walked through the park to the old well. Two pickup trucks were there, loaded with fruits and vegetables. The man selling them said he brings them back from a farmer's market in Atlanta. I calculated the drive at two to three hours, one way! One of the drivers said he had passed me in Cannon that morning.

At the old well, I met John Whitmire and Ralph Jordan. "For the last two days," John told me, "I have been the oldest person in town." A man two years his senior had just died. Ralph informed me that John walks between two and four miles a day.

I noted that Bowman is a two-watertank town. John spoke of moving to Bowman in 1906, at the age of six, because it was the only place with a school at the time. He reminisced, "They used to gather around this well with horses and buggies. A lot of mules and horses have been watered at this well. There used to be benches all around it where folks would sit."

I could see the old grooves in the posts holding up the roof over the well. There are fewer Charleston-type freestanding benches now and no one seems to have time to occupy them. John also shared with me that all the buildings around the square had been wood until they had burned and were rebuilt; even the bank had burned up.

Not far out of Bowman, forsythia was blooming by an antique house with a fine chinaberry tree. I passed the tree, then turned around, and pedaled into the wind a few hundred yards to take a picture. Wow, what a tailwind I'd had! You don't often realize you have a tailwind when you are being blown along by it.

That tailwind assisted me right through Dewy Rose, another town along the railroad line. Most of the signs were of granite. There were white flowering trees and shrubs, yellow daffodils, forsythia in bloom, and many trees growing vast crops of mistletoe. Occasionally, I saw a pecan grove or a pecan tree shading a house.

I passed the Davis Floral Company's greenhouses and was reminded of a story about Nancy Raposo, a rider on the Race Across America (RAAM). She had trained by riding her bicycle on rollers in a greenhouse several hours a day to acclimate herself to hot weather. She lived in Rhode Island and needed to prepare for the hot desert atmosphere of late summer. Nancy's strategy was to prepare for the heat, but not try to race in desert heat. She just planned to get through it fast, without overstressing her body. Later in the race, she had more strength than others. Her support crew followed in vehicles. The training and support paid off; Nancy won first women's place in RAAM.

The granite signs reminded me that I was on the Piedmont Plateau, where most of Georgia's largest cities are. The northern part of Georgia is older, geologically, than the plateau area. Geologists have learned that many upheavals and erosions occurred on the land before Georgia took its present form of mountains in the north, plateau in the middle, and coastal plain in the south. The mountains at the northwest corner are part of the Appalachian Plateau. The northeastern Georgia mountains are the southern section of the Blue Ridge Mountains. Between these two mountain ranges is a series of valleys and ridges that are a southern extension of the Smoky Mountains.

Where I was pedaling, the line between the mountainous north and the rolling Piedmont Plateau is less distinct than the 400 foot fall line which separates the plateau from the plain and runs across Georgia from Columbus to Macon and on to Augusta. This fall line marks the coastline of an earlier geologic era. Rich clays and sands, such as the famous red clay and white kaolin, are visible in the area of the dropoff.

Underneath one-fourth of Georgia's land are ancient crystalline rocks like granite. Granite forms Stone Mountain near Atlanta and is so plentiful in the Elberton area that it provides a major industry.

On the outskirts of the town of Elberton, I met Kenneth Allgood as he came out of his office and got into his pickup. He invited me to photograph his granite cutting, lifting, and polishing operation that stood near the road. It was an opportunity I couldn't resist. A large circular saw, cooled continuously by water, squealed through a block of granite, accompanied by flying dust and mist. I watched, fascinated, and took lots of pictures.

A short pedal time brought me into the town itself. Three years ago I had visited the Elberton Granite Museum, along with hundreds of other cyclists on BRAG. The museum, usually closed on Mondays, had opened specifically for the BRAG tourers. I'd spent hours inside with friends, looking at tools and films. The local use of granite impressed me. I've always liked hardware stores, so the methodology and tools of the granite quarry, cutting, and polishing kept my attention.

BRAG entered Elberton on Highway 77, a route that passed the Georgia Guidestones, granite monoliths set up like Stonehenge in England. The impressive stones were inscribed with a message of peace for future generations, in twelve languages. I remembered that they seemed incongruous, stuck out in a Georgia field, but very peaceful. Perhaps Stonehenge had once seemed incongruous, too.

I continued south, stopping for lunch at McDonald's. It, too, had a fine granite sign in addition to its normal arches. I also noted granite markers for homes, businesses, farms, and even a trailer. Instead of logging trucks, so common in other parts of Georgia, this area had trucks that hauled granite. There were even granite trash heaps. Granite was everywhere! Almost 90 percent of the granite business, however, rests in cemeteries.

It was a great day for bicycling. The tailwind continued to push me through Riceboro, where the largest house belonged to M. L. Rice and where John Rice & Son ran an auto repair place.

I had to outrun a dog that had its ruff up and came on in spite of its owner's yells. I had the tailwind and a slight downgrade, so it wasn't much trouble to get away, even with my load. I could do without dogs on uphills, though!

One of the few things I do not carry is a gun. I do have Halt, a product designed to ward off dogs. Most mail carriers tote it. I've seldom used it because I don't want to spray a mace-like product on someone's pet. It's also a bit tricky because you need to be upwind of the spray or you get a dose yourself — not a pleasant experience. I've never had cause to use it against a human. People have been much too nice. Anyway, I've learned that everyone knows everyone else in rural areas. As long as I behave and remain alert, it is unlikely that anyone will bother me. I think Roosevelt put it well — the greatest fear is fear itself. I think fear paralyzes worse than polio because it is both mental and emotional, and less obvious than physical paralysis. Fear is easier to cure, however, because it is self-inflicted, and therefore, self-removable. Unfortunately, we humans are not quick to look to ourselves for the causes of our woes.

By the time I crossed the Broad River into Lincoln County, it was after 2:00 P.M. and I'd pedaled about 50 miles. I soon entered Chennault Community and crossed Ford Creek. I passed Chennault Plantation, site of the Gold Train Robbery, where the entire Confederate Treasury was attacked. The house is now restored and the plantation runs hunting tours.

The afternoon was clear, sunny, warm, and a wonderful one in which to roll downhill along the sparsely traveled road. A beautifully restored old home on my left had white columns and an upper, as well as lower, front porch. On the right spread a great meadow for horseback riding with a few jumps set out.

Occasionally, I'd go down a steep hill and wonder whether I'd come off the Piedmont, but there would soon be an elevation. Like the Savannah River not far away to my left, I continued seaward. The steep descent at Fishing Creek took me all the way to 28 miles per hour. To pay for my fun, I crawled up the other side at three miles an hour. Pilots, physicists, and cyclists all agree that what goes up must come down. But cyclists also know that what goes down must go up again!

Spanish moss clung to branches more frequently as the miles rolled away. The wild plums that I enjoyed eating as a kid were in bloom and a field of daffodils smelled wonderful.

Finally, I cranked the pedals up the last hill into Lincolnton. It would not have been a tough hill in the morning, but now there were 70 miles on my legs. I was relieved to see the city limits sign and know I had arrived.

Two women were discussing plants and trees in the front yard of a large, white-columned home with an expanse of shrubs and trees. They looked up and waved. I stopped. They realized they had mistaken me for someone else who often rides a loaded bicycle. As we talked, they said they wouldn't recommend the motel, and the only camping was at Elijah Clark State Park, eight miles east.

I wasn't anxious to pedal one inch further. Secretly, I wished they would invite me to camp in the yard, but knew the idea would never occur to them. I waved cheerily, but inwardly had to dredge up the energy to go the extra miles. One of the other things I've learned about touring by bike is that stopping has certain rules. *Rule 1:* You can ride as far as your head thinks you have to go; if you think 90 miles, you can go them. If, however, two extra miles are added at the end, they seem impossible. To get anywhere one's will must prove stronger than one's muscles in their perpetual tug-o-war. Therefore, *Rule 2:* Once you stop, it's hard to get going again.

I followed the ladies' directions to the Home Cafe. It was closed until 5:00 P.M., so I used the quarter-hour to pedal around the block and look at this town perched on the side of a hill.

It was 70 degrees, according to the bank clock, and I'd traveled 71 miles. At the police station, I asked again about the motel. The officer on duty thought I'd prefer the state park. Looking at his shoes, he said, "Well, the motel is run by a family from India."

I thought about my pleasant experience at the Days Inn and asked him for more information.

"I wouldn't stay there," he replied, continuing to regard his shoes. "The state park is wonderful. It is only eight miles and most of that is downhill." I thanked him. The situation was clear. I would pedal eight more miles tonight. Groaning inside, I rested my helmeted head on my handlebars. I tried to think positively. Maybe after eating supper and resting awhile I would feel better; he had said it was mostly downhill.

I slowly cranked back to the cafe. Thankfully, the two women inside turned the "Closed" sign around and unlocked the door. Supper was ready on the steam table. I selected meatloaf, mashed potatoes, a little gravy, turnip greens, green beans, and cornbread. Everything was home cooked and tasted fresh.

Typically curious and friendly, the owner, Lynn, talked with me until other people came in. We discussed her nice restaurant and she told me how she came to have it. She had wanted to buy Home Cafe when it was on the market over a year ago, but the owner didn't like some of the terms of her offer and refused it. A week later someone else bought the cafe, disappointing her mightily. Only a few months ago, however, the new owner found it too much and sold the restaurant to Lynn. People called in orders, some came for carry out, and others like me stayed to eat and chat. Lynn and her husband (very supportive of her Cafe project, she said) had grown up in Augusta, but lived in the country near Lincolnton. She delivers dinners to some of the shut-ins on her way home.

Lynn and her husband believe there is much more to Georgia than many natives realize. "Georgia has it all, even a canyon to go with the mountains, coast, cities, and Piedmont," she said. "We like Georgia. We live here, take our vacations here, and wonder why so many people don't realize how interesting, historic, and beautiful Georgia is. You should see Price's store; it is the oldest continuously operating country store in Georgia. Ask Janie who runs it to direct you back to the Augusta highway so you won't have to go out of your way to come back through Lincolnton."

After the rest and supper, I did feel better and took off to pedal the eight miles to the state park. I stopped once to read an historical marker about the Petersburg Road, which weaves across the current road to Augusta several times. The Petersburg Road was used by the Indians and pioneer settlers moving up and down near the Savannah River. Cotton and tobacco were transported along this road from Petersburg to Augusta.

It was almost sunset when I crossed Soap Creek, passed a Tory Pond historical marker, and turned at the entry road of Elijah Clark Memorial State Park. I startled a pair of large white-tailed deer which leapt a four-foot barbed-wire fence with plenty of clearance and disappeared in the forest while another stood still at the edge of the underbrush, watching. The rays of the setting sun measured longer shadows, and I knew I'd better get the tent pitched before it got too dark to see.

The campsite stood on a small peninsula, jutting into the Clarks Hill reservoir of the Savannah River. I unloaded the panniers into the tent, took a hot shower in the bath house, and crawled in. I stretched my legs and lay quietly, on comfortable pinestraw under the tent floor, content to be on the road again.

After decompressing from the long but lovely ride, I got up again. I ate a few apricots for dessert and then plugged a long extension cord into the electric box. Turning on my four-watt night light, I set up the computer to begin recording the notes I'd dictated.

Later, readjusting the light, I dropped it and broke the bulb. Time for sleep! On one last trip to the bathhouse, I met a woman camping in a nearby trailer with her husband. We chatted about my trip and she gave me the weather forecast for overnight showers. Oh, well. My tent was dry and I hoped for another beautiful day as we said our good-nights.

I took one last glimpse at the distant dark lake, then zipped my tent shut for the first time in several years.

Elijah Clark Memorial State Park, Friday, March 8

When I awoke, wind was shaking the tent. I looked out. There was no sign of rain — yea! I cozily lay abed and dozed until it was good light, then packed up deliberately. I pedaled away from the park that had been as nice as advertised, but now I was headed for a country-ham-and-homemade-biscuit breakfast at Price's Store, about ten miles toward Augusta. Unfortunately, the rain did come but only in the form of drizzle for a few miles. It was overcast and cold — but not rainy — for the rest of the day.

Not far from the camp, on GA 220, pedaling up from the Soap Creek causeway-bridge, I stopped short of the crest of the hill. I couldn't believe my eyes. There were two buffalo in a pasture! They glowered shaggily at me as I walked a little closer for a photo. Nearby, dogs began to bark urgently, so I returned to the bike and continued. Climbing the next hill a mile away, I could still hear the ear-splitting bark of one of the dogs. Despite the fascination of the buffalo, I was glad to be away.

Instead of continuing on Route 220 to the Augusta highway, I proceeded straight on a spur, Double Branches Road. Someone was burning trash wood, filling the air with the wonderful smell of wood-smoke. A few more miles past the Ashton-Barden Road, which also leads to the Augusta highway, I looked over fields which cattle were sharing with Canada geese, flocks of robins, and a multitude of meadowlarks.

Soon I came upon Price's Store. I leaned my bike against a bench, removed helmet, wool cap, gloves, and read the temperature above the gas pump at 43 degrees. I opened the plastic-covered screen door and went inside the wood-frame building, which listed slightly.

A marvelous pot-bellied stove stood in the back with two chairs and two well-worn benches around it. Even though it was after ten o'clock, three people huddled around the stove, like a mirage of old country store tales.

Helping myself to a decaffeinated Diet Coke and a ham biscuit wrapped in plastic, I sat near the stove, eating quietly, listening and observing. The proprietor, a lady I soon knew to be Jane McWhorter, waited on customers who were buying a whole carful of food. They took four heads of cabbage Jane had picked that morning before making biscuits.

Rousing from the revery and comfortable conversation, I shook myself back into the present. Breakfast had been nice. I took some photos of the people and the stove, then followed the mailman outside to get directions to the Augusta highway.

It was cold and raw outside, especially since I'd cooled off from pedaling. I retreated inside where I, too, huddled by the stove until the customers left. Then I introduced myself to Jane and asked about the store.

She was a direct descendent of its founder, John Marshall Price. As current owner, she guarded the "same as usual" atmosphere. Top shelves and walls were lined with tins and implements, valuable antiques. General merchandise, gas, fishing supplies, and feed were for sale. Since its beginning in 1897, Price's has had a reputation for selling everything you need in life, "from cradle to coffin," as the saying goes. I'll bet you could look all over Augusta for some things found only in Price's Store!

Jane told me how family members would travel to New York and North Carolina to buy the clothing and furniture which stocked the store in the days before traveling salesmen or drummers. We talked about the pot-bellied stove and the old-fashioned picture it presents.

Jane said she wished she had more time to sit and visit, but she does everything at the store herself, with occasional help from her daughter when she's home from college. "I really love running the store," she said, smiling. She still expects people to ask for what they need so she can wait on them. I certainly had found a piece of Georgia as it once was.

I mentioned the concoction cooking on a two-eye electric stove. The good-smelling pot, Jane told me, was peanuts boiling. I'd never eaten boiled peanuts, so she took them off the heat and gave me a few in a bowl. As soon as they were cool enough, I found out how delicious they are and why homemade signs along Georgia highways advertise them!

I asked Jane about the buffalo I'd seen. She said it could be that people were trying different types of farming. A couple recently bought a hog farm that went under and planned to raise ostriches. "Just for the feathers?" I wanted to know. She explained that every part of the bird was commercially useful.

I finally did some real shopping, asking about a replacement bulb for my tent light. All she had were standard light bulbs so I sat a while longer. While other customers came in, I read several newspaper articles. Two hours flew by.

Thinking of the weather, I was tempted to ask if I could camp there the rest of the day and overnight in her back yard. However, I'd promised Liz and George Brewton I'd try to reach Louisville on the weekend so George and his friends could ride out to meet me and we would have more time to visit. I knew I'd have to come back to Price's Store and Double Branches Community, for there was no time to visit here longer. I also wanted to see Bussey Point, where Jane told me I would find a U.S. Army Corps of Engineers wildlife park and a large wild turkey farm, as well as hiking and horseback riding trails and a quiet camping area. The little region seemed packed with surprises!

I departed reluctantly. Down the road apiece, I found my way past a group of trailers which was home to the people buying that carload of food. Soon after, I turned onto the Augusta Road, GA 47, and continued downhill.

I crossed a bridge into Columbia County where a sign of welcome said "CSRA Trail County," which Jane had told me meant Central Savannah River Area. The Bartram Trail, which I had first heard of in Rabun County, crossed the highway. William Bartram was a famous naturalist who traveled extensively in Georgia in the 1700s. He left such detailed notes about places he visited that his routes are marked.

After about ten miles of pedaling, I entered the town of Leah, and I felt hungry. I went into a store where barbecue was advertised, but the girl said her father had passed away recently. "I'll start cooking tomorrow," she told me. It seems I found a story wherever I turned on this trip!

I got back on the bike and took off again. It was almost one o'clock when I found the Ridge Road Bait & Tackle Cafe and Grocery. I ordered a hamburger with lettuce, tomato, and mustard, and took a decaffeinated Diet Coke out of the cooler. As I was about to sit down in a booth, a man asked where I was coming from. I told him. Tom Hardin introduced himself and his "Yankee" friend, Bob Soncrant. They invited me to sit with them.

Tom said his family had been residents of the area since 1736 when they had migrated from Hardin County, Kentucky. I'd thought most people migrated from east to west, and decided to keep my ears open on the subject. His ancestors are buried in Columbia County nearby. Bob said it was true he was a Yankee, but he enjoyed living in Georgia.

Tom told me about a hobby that I found very interesting. He finds old, forgotten cemeteries and copies the names off the stones. Sometimes he checks the area around a new find to learn if any family members still live there. "I like tramping in the woods and finding things," he summarized.

Once again I'd found pleasant company. I had to go, even in such gray weather, so I excused myself and continued toward Augusta.

The traffic got heavier as I approached the city, hill by hill. The day also got cooler as the afternoon slid under my wheels. Continuing on Route 104, which became Washington Road in Martinez, I phoned Augusta House and talked with Betty Hoopes, who was expecting me. She gave me detailed directions. I arrived late in the afternoon, after a few hills too many and one other encounter.

With only a few blocks to go, I stopped in response to a yell. The way he sounded, it had to be a bicyclist. A man came running around the corner and announced that he was Sy Winiker.

"It is so rare to see a loaded touring bike in Augusta, I just had to meet you. How old are you? And a woman too! Congratulations, I'm proud to meet you!" he tumbled on. "I'm going to ride to New England in June, then go out west. I've toured a lot and can't wait to get on the road again."

He continued, asking questions about the bike, what I was carrying, where I came from, where I was going. We talked about packing for long, self-contained trips. He carries a gallon container for water and, after filling it and buying his evening groceries, camps just anywhere — but usually not in a campground.

"You're really something," he added. "I'm glad to meet you. Good luck! I have to continue my five mile-walk. I ride about 20 miles when I get time on the weekends. I'm an electrician."

Finally we parted, but he caught up with me while I was reading an historical marker a couple of blocks away and gave me his card. He said, "I'm only 57, wonderful to see another bike tourist. Have a good trip."

I had stopped to read about the Jones House, home of a former Georgia governor. Crossing the street, I turned into the driveway of Augusta House. Built in 1928, the English Tudor mansion, located near the Augusta Country Club, is the largest home in Augusta, and is now run as a bed and breakfast. Its 26 rooms are constructed of costly imported materials, beautiful paneling, leaded and stained-glass windows, marble fireplaces, and wondrous tiled baths. Three acres of gardens provide a quiet setting.

The smell of old boxwood enveloped me as I rang the bell. Betty Hoopes welcomed me and introduced her husband, Sarge, an antique dealer who specializes in wicker.

We spent a lovely evening sharing stories of our various adventures, sitting comfortably and informally in the wicker room, where the floor is tiled in black and white. The fireplace warmed us as the sun sank and darkened the windows.

The Hoopes had only owned the house a few years. They had enjoyed filling it with their special collections of arrowheads, prints, and antique furniture. We talked about antiques, wood carving, remodeling, importing rugs, running a bed and breakfast, and, of course, what it is like to be in Augusta every spring for the Masters Golf Tournament, held when the dogwood and azaleas are in bloom.

The Hoopes told stories of how far people came for the Masters — from Japan and many other countries, and from all parts of the United States and Europe. No one understands how the tickets get around, for there are never enough and they may not be sold — they are inherited. (Later, I asked a few Georgians who said they give tickets to their friends when they can't go. People who have tickets go, every year, all their lives.)

I had not realized that the Masters Golf Course is seldom used except for the tournament. Entry is prohibited at other times of the year.

Even during the tournament, cameras are permitted only to the press. The course was built on the site of a former nursery, a partial explanation for the beauty of the ancient azaleas and other trees and shrubs. Like so many others during the Masters, the Hoopes rent their whole house, once a year, to the staff of *Golf Digest*. Betty laughingly admitted they get more money that way, and she doesn't have to prepare breakfast!

Augusta, Saturday, March 9

I awoke, still lulled by the ambiance and good company. The Hoopes were so hospitable and such enjoyable company, I couldn't have found better rest during my visit to Augusta.

Early morning rain once again added to my reluctance to move out. My late start, though, was accelerated by a long roll downhill, dropping over 300 feet to the plain, which brought me to downtown Augusta and the restored Cotton Exchange Building.

At the height of the cotton boom, Augusta was second only to Memphis in trade volume. Built in 1886, the Cotton Exchange Building was the center of every part of the cotton trade. The building, restored in 1988, contains a permanent exhibit called "Cotton Pickin' Deals" that explains the importance of cotton. It includes the original trading chalk board with a day's quotes.

After exploring the building and admiring its exterior, I strolled along River Walk on the other side of the levee and finally began to pedal. At first, I stayed parallel to the river and headed south on Broad Street. I went too far, though, to the bridge leading to South Carolina, and had to turn back. Then I headed west for Louisville and reached the road to Hephzibah, which put me in the country again.

In the distance, I could see white kaolin cliffs gleaming in the sun along the fall line. Kaolin, the most valuable of Georgia clays, was discovered and mined in colonial days for shipment to England to make Wedgewood pottery. Now it is used in paper products and cosmetics.

I rode past red clay banks and pine trees, and pedaled through Blythe, where an old-fashioned aeroplane — that looked and sounded like a Tiger Moth — flew overhead. (The next day, Julian Veatch, mayor of Louisville, told me a small airfield near Blythe, called Pea Patch, was home to many unusual propeller-driven flying machines.)

Rolling into Keysville, I got another feeling of de`ja vu and realized that I had also been there during one of the BRAG rides. As I stood in the local store and ate popcorn and an apple, I figured out it was about three years ago that we had pedaled through Keysville. Outside again, the town looked quiet and the road was deserted. Yet I could see, in my mind's eye, the townspeople selling watermelon, fish sandwiches, and cookies while they laughed and talked with the bicyclists clad in their vivid outfits. There I had met and talked with Andrew Young, then mayor of Atlanta, and his wife, while devouring fish sandwiches.

A male friend had told me of stopping at a house up the road to get some water. He had overheard two old men sitting in rockers on the porch. One said to the other, "Did you ever see so many women wearing their girdles on the outside?" He was referring to the lycra bicycling shorts worn by men and women alike! The story spread quickly and one could see where it was being told by watching the ripples of laughter pass over the crowd.

I stood under the storefront and looked again at the empty road. We had been a cultural shock to the town, but we had paid our way. One of the organizers estimated that when the 2,000 BRAG pedalers crossed Georgia, they "dropped" forty to fifty thousand dollars a day. Someone else told me we more than doubled the population of many counties while we pedaled across them.

I reentered the store and returned to the present, worried about being late to meet my friend George Brewton, who was riding to meet me. Glancing at the wall clock, I saw I should be meeting him in a few minutes — over twenty miles ahead. Then the door opened and George stepped through it!

"It was such a wondrous day," he bellowed, greeting me, "that I couldn't wait, and set out earlier than expected. This is the finest day for bicycling we've had this year."

Indeed! The afternoon had improved to be a sunny, relatively warm, and glorious day, far beyond my expectations at dawn when I had peered out the window for an eyewitness weather report and seen nothing but rain. Eagerly, we hopped aboard our bikes and turned back the way George had just come.

While we pedaled, George told stories about the houses with open spaces, breezeways, that he called dog runs. I learned that one elegant brick home, which had an unfinished wall, was in that condition because the drug-dealing owner had been incarcerated before its completion.

When we reached Vidette, I realized it was the town where a group of us had taken photos, standing in the window of a vacant storefront during one of the BRAG rides. I guess I kept having these flashbacks because half the time on BRAG, we didn't really know — or care — where we were! BRAG is so social, and people ride and talk so fast, that they just enjoy pedaling and seldom look at the map or read the signs.

Even though each day's BRAG route is in a small book of arranged maps, north often isn't the same direction from page to page, and I'd often been disoriented. Now I remembered ,from local landmarks, where we had halted, but not how locations related to each other.

George had called Liz and asked her to meet us on the road in her car. She did so, taking all my panniers. Unloaded at last, George and I rode side by side when there was no traffic, happily talking of friends and our activities in the League of American Wheelmen, a national cycling organization. I guess we talked more than we pedaled, for Liz came back to find how we had progressed when we were still two miles from their home!

I'd first met George during a bicycle ride that followed a route described in a book, tracing Sherman's march to the sea during the Civil War. Everyone, including the author, got lost using the directions from the book that we were promoting! Apparently, neither editor nor author was familiar with standard cue sheet notational systems used in America. The author had ridden the route with groups of kids for ten years, and if he got lost, he considered it a route revision. We had kept our humor and enjoyed the lark.

Bicyclists who don't join clubs or lead rides may not realize the hours required to produce a reliable cue sheet and clearly marked route for a single day's ride. Ride instructions for a big ride of several hundred people are driven and pedaled several times, by car and bicycle, to check for accuracy. Some ride organizers even drive the route the night before a big event so they can inform the bicyclists of any changes, such as construction, closures, or improvements.

Later, I got to know George better when we, and a dozen other bicyclists, participated in a three-week tour from Portland, Maine, to Orlando, Florida, raising funds for charity and supporting bicycling education. We had ridden together during that tour; I could hear more of

George's stories that way. Pedaling along now, we discussed an invitation to join a people-to-people tour of China that we both had declined.

During my two nights with George and Liz, they saw to it that I was thoroughly entertained. Sunday was indeed busy. In the morning, I did trip chores and laundry, demonstrated to George how to cook a chain, and inspected his bike shop shed. Then Liz took me on a visit to Fulgrum Industries, Inc., where she is vice president. In the afternoon, I took photos of Louisville and we met friends.

Market House, Louisville

As we toured the Fulgrum plant, Liz described the wood chip mills and other heavy equipment they design, manufacture, and install around the world for the wood processing industry. There were several people at work that Sunday. When Liz introduced me as another bicyclist, one man asked if I was as crazy as George. Liz confirmed, "More so!" The man continued that he thought us as silly as runners. "Why run if nobody is chasing you?" he muttered as he walked away, shaking his head. Liz and I just laughed.

The company, established in 1956, is located a few miles south of Louisville in Wadley, formerly called Shake Rag. The town grew where the train tracks for the Savannah-to-Atlanta Central of Georgia Railroad crossed US 1. George's mother often went out to shake a rag to stop and board the Nancy Hanks train for a day of shopping in Atlanta. Fulgrum Industries, Inc. has 175 employees and annual sales over $25 million, proof that small Southern towns can indeed support very profitable businesses.

I had pedaled away from the perimeter of Georgia, inland and southwest from the Savannah River, for two reasons. I wanted to see the Brewtons and I wanted to visit Louisville, the first permanent site of the capital of Georgia, from 1796 to 1805. The Old Market on Broad Street was built back in 1758.

During my visit to Louisville on Sunday afternoon, Liz introduced me to Mayor Julian Veatch, who told me about the town bell. Cast in 1772 in France for a convent in New Orleans, the bell had been looted by pirates from a ship and sold in Savannah to the people of Louisville. It called the townfolk in case of fire, announcements, or danger. It had hung in Market House, at the center of town, from the mid-1700s until a recent disappearance. The mayor announced that if the bell was returned safely, there would be no penalty and no one would ever know the culprit. The fine old bell returned as mysteriously as it had disappeared.

Mayor Veatch and his wife Elinor were jolly company. Bicycling is about the only thing he doesn't do. The mayor is also a veterinarian; his CB nickname is K-9 Doc. Elinor Veatch grew up in Columbus. It turns out she went to school with Zeke Gaines, who married my friend Courtney, of Savannah. We also knew some of the same people in Clayton.

We were joined by Robert and Jean Cooper, friends of George and Liz. Robert is a design engineer at Fulgrum Industries, and an avid bicyclist. He designs sawmills that are less expensive than others because of a special patent on the teeth of a circular saw that allows it to saw a thin line, almost as narrow as a band saw, thus saving wood. Robert and George are the bicycle club of Louisville — so far. I have faith that their enthusiasm will add to the numbers! We enjoyed a very entertaining afternoon.

With all the new people I'd met, the places I'd seen before on BRAG, and the friends I'd revisited already, the state of Georgia began to remind me of Switzerland. In that country, it is also impossible to

travel without meeting someone you know, or someone who knows
your friends.

Louisville, Monday, March 11

Early Monday morning, Liz and George bade me goodbye and I
pedaled out on GA 17 toward Midville. Though the morning was sunny,
it was cold at first light, in the low 30s. After George guided me to the
edge of town and I'd pedaled almost an hour, I came to Old Town
Plantation at the top of a hill and read the historical marker. Off came a
sweater and out came the camera before I continued through the lovely
morning along a ridge on the north side of the Ogeechee River. The river
spreads to swamp and marsh as it reaches the Atlantic on the south side
of Savannah.

When I pedaled down to the Bark Camp Creek Bridge, I leaned my
bike against the rail and went under the bridge to make a cyclist's use of
outdoor "facilities." Then I sat on the rail in the sun, eating an apple and
watching a hawk. I couldn't figure out what variety it was, perhaps because
I was too busy recalling the dinner George had prepared the night before
— smothered venison steak, with butter beans from last year's garden and
potatoes with his special no-fat gravy. George doesn't hunt, but a friend
gives him deer. A pleasant visit with good friends — nice memories.

I paralleled the Ogeechee River course. I'd intended to eat at
Dyer's Cafe in Midville, but it had closed. I rode on to Millen, established
in 1852. Hardee's provided welcome pancakes. While I was eating, a
woman invited me to stay at her home or at least to stop by for some
good, cold well water. Having told Courtney Gaines I'd reach Savannah
that day, I felt committed to continuing but agreed to call on another visit.
I'd made another acquaintance!

When I left Hardee's, I turned near a hair salon called "Tangles" and
pedaled through more pine forests and farm pastures. At Scarboro, I recalled
stopping on two bike tours to see the church and country store, now closed. On
one of those occasions, I had jumped into the Ogeechee for a cooling
swim. This time it was too cold for a swim, but I saw something else. Turkey
vultures, feeding along the road, flew away from a deer carcass before I got
close enough for a photo. There must have been a dozen of them.

As I rode on, the road flattened and flattened, more marshy places
appeared, and Marsh Creek was far out of its banks. Oak and live oak

with palmetto undergrowth spread between cotton and corn fields. Some farmers had begun spring plowing or were riding their tractors for whatever reason. From Rocky Ford, the route toward Cooperville was new to me. Winter wheat looked like beautiful, tall green grass; George had taught me to recognize it.

A big field of plastic strips caught my attention and I stopped to question the farmer about what the field contained. "Only fertilizer now, under the plastic," he said.

"What will you be growing later?" I asked.

"Watermelons," he answered abruptly, obviously a good Southerner who believed that people generally minded their own business. Although it took a few questions, I learned that several varieties of watermelon would be planted and the wholesalers would drive their empty 18-wheelers there and buy about 20 truckloads in June.

Continuing, I watched a falcon circling over a field and saw several woodpeckers. I passed a large plant of the King Finishing Company, a division of Spartan Mills, dyers and finishers of quality fabrics.

I reached Cooperville Community about 1:00 P.M. Hungry after 55 miles, I was only halfway to Savannah and running late. At the Paradise Motel, on the shortest bicycling route from Louisville to Savannah as it crossed Highway 301, I ate again, a fine lunch of fried fish, greens, black-eyed peas, and rice. I was glad that George had told me about the place because it was not on my map.

I poured the second glass of sweet tea into my water bottle, made a few phone calls, and continued through Oliver and Egypt. I was pushed by a tailwind over quite flat terrain, very different from the morning route when I had traveled a ridge road through woods and slightly rolling cotton, corn and watermelon fields. I was now pedaling a straight road with water in its ditches and live oak along the roadside, often draped with yellow jasmine blooms.

Some trees, like the magnolia, are so common here, and so familiar to me, that I seldom notice them. A magnolia tree grows in my neighbor's yard in Washington, D.C., and my mother's country place had a large one which I topped to make it bushy. A friend had teased me about it, saying that I had ruined the tree. She kept it up for about five years until another branch took over as the top and the luxurious tree filled out. Then she presented me with a certificate, drawn to resemble her garden club awards!

Later in the afternoon, the road was straighter and the woods contained cypress, laurel, and palmetto, as well as pines and oak-shrubs, garlanded by more blooming yellow jasmine. I called Courtney from Guyton (established in 1838) and told her I was 19 miles north of Pooler. It was getting quite late, and it became increasingly clear that, with the load I was carrying and with my 11-to-14 mile-per-hour rate of travel, I would not reach Savannah before dark. Courtney, a friend and bicycling buddy, met me nine miles west of Savannah at the Pooler McDonald's. The sun had set before we got bike and baggage in her station wagon and headed off through the night to Savannah.

When Courtney and I reached the shopping center south of Savannah, we headed for The Mill, a homemade bakery, brewery, and eatery. There, I met David Moynihan, Tannia Corley, Joe Drescher, president of the Coastal Bicycle Touring Club, and Mary Anne Scheer, chairperson of the end-of-the-road party for BRAG. We had coffee and dessert and, naturally, we talked about bicycling, eating, and plans for the end-of-the-road party for the next Bicycle Ride Across Georgia.

That annual ride would begin outside Atlanta and guide 2,000 bicyclists through the state. It would include overnight stops at Lake Jackson, Milledgeville, Dublin, Eastman, Vidalia, and Statesboro, and would finish six days later in Savannah. It would be a tour of 350 miles — about the same distance I'd traveled so far, having culminated my first week on the road with the 105-mile trek from Louisville to Pooler.

I'd gotten to know Joe Drescher on River Street in Savannah last August, waiting around for the Race Across America riders to cross the finish line of the toughest bicycle race anywhere. They had pedaled from Irvine, California, to Savannah in eight to ten days. Bob Fourney was the first man, and Nancy Raposo the first woman to finish that year. A Swiss man, Philippe Vetterli, was among those who finished successfully and received an award. Everyone who completes RAAM is a winner and receives the coveted RAAM ring!

Several months later I received a letter from a Swiss friend who had seen me on Swiss television, talking with the RAAM Swiss crew — a small-world adventure! Are there causes we neither see nor understand behind effects that we label coincidence?

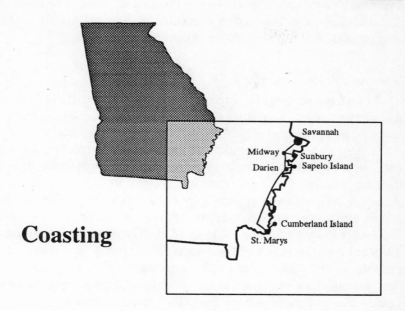

Coasting

Savanah, Tuesday, March 12

Every visit to Savannah I've made during the past five years has included a stay at the home of Courtney Gaines. This time, as usual, she made me feel welcome. I had a real rest day. Courtney went about her normal activities while I read, sat on the porch, telephoned, and napped. We piled our bicycles into her car in mid-afternoon and drove, along a route we had pedaled many times, to Skidaway Island, where Courtney planned to build a home in The Landings, a private community. Once inside, we pulled out our bicycles and explored the streets and the walking/bicycle paths that gave us views of the lots from all sides. We looked in detail at several lots, and when Courtney told me I chose the same lot as her real estate advisors, it made me feel good about my judgment.

I took photos of a pool full of mergansers, watched an anhinga dry its wings, and had a close look through binoculars at the first red-headed woodpecker of this tour. Though we didn't travel far on our bikes, we did shake the kinks out of our muscles. We did some research, visited an outer island of Georgia, and worked up an appetite. Supper at The Mill was just as good as dessert had been the night before.

Savannah, Wednesday, March 13

From Courtney's home, south of DeRenne, I pedaled into Old Savannah on a route which runs along Habersham and Lincoln. It was drizzling when I started; I arrived at the Savannah Visitor's Center in a downpour.

Where could I leave the bike? At the far end of the parking lot, near the Central of Georgia Railroad restaurant car, I saw a spot sheltered from the rain. I locked the bicycle there and boarded the Savannah Heritage Association Grey Line tour bus. It feeds part of its profits back into the restoration of historic homes, being the same group that restored the Isaiah Davenport House, built from 1815 to 1820. The threat of demolition in 1955 got the restoration of Davenport House going, and spurred the growth of the Historic Savannah Foundation. I've also heard that destruction of the old city market to construct a large parking lot so ignited Savannah citizens that support for restoration took wings.

The two-mile-square, old-town area is the largest preservation area in America. A bicycle offers a grand way to see it. The closest camping is at Skidaway State Park, but motels abound in the city. Bicycle paths about half the width of a parking space are posted with signs to facilitate travel — especially in and out of the city. More important, they must be policed, for I saw no one misusing them as parking areas. Although I had visited River Street numerous times, I never really appreciated its community feeling until I hung out there for a Race Across America finish. From all over America, racers, crews and organizers, were so delighted by Savannah hospitality that many bicyclists believe RAAM has found a permanent home for its finish line on River Street. Savannah is a bicycle-friendly town.

On this day, I was glad to sit on the bus and be told what I was seeing, even though I had toured Savannah before. I am always ready to spend a day on River Street, eating pralines from River Street Sweets (better than I found in New Orleans), prowling in shops or in the Ships of the Sea Museum.

As the bus moved through the historic streets, I found myself thinking again about my own relationship to Georgia history. Not long after Savannah was founded in 1733, its English residents' quiet, urban life was disturbed by a new element. Feisty, Scotch-Irish people from the backwoods drove their wagons through Savannah's dirt streets. Barely literate, rough-and-ready, but hard-working, they sold their fresh produce to the cultivated English, who dubbed the whip-wielding intruders "crackers." I used to think the term had something to do with soda crackers. Instinct, rather than knowledge, had led me to rebut all comments about my being a "Georgia cracker" with a sweet smile and the reply, "No, I'm a Georgia peach." Peaches are still a major crop in the state. As a child, I ate so many in the summer the fuzz didn't irritate my mouth, but I couldn't stop the juice from running down my chin.

Then a few years ago, reading *Eden on the Marsh,* by Edward Chan Sieg, made me realize that, being descended from Scotch-Irish and German people who had been in Georgia since before the Revolutionary War, I might well be a "cracker." But, when challenged, I still claim to be a peach.

Our tour guide interrupted my revery with remarks about Factors Walk. "Factor" is an old word for agent or broker. It was a term used in the cotton business for the individuals who bought and sold cotton — much like today's stock brokers. Without computers or telephones, they had to walk among the offices and warehouses to conduct business. Hence the term, "Factors Walk." The warehouses have been converted to shops at the street level and to hotels, restaurants, or offices above.

River Street still has daily train traffic. Bicycles travel on the sidewalk by the riverside park which replaced the wharfs. The original ballast-stone surface of the streets, which would shake a car apart if it moved faster than walking speed, helps control automobile traffic. Our guide talked about the cobble pavement and the stone walls near River Street, where the Hyatt Hotel is built over the street. He said the cobblestones originally came from Belgium. Geology students frequently study the stone walls because they contain every type of stone known in the world. Sailing ships brought the stones for ballast when carrying light, bulky cargo or when the cargo failed to fill the ship to a safe weight for sailing. It occurred to me, thinking about these ballast stones, that the colonists were not isolated in America. Shipping under sail connected world cultures through commerce much as the media does today. The difference was the time. News or gossip probably traveled faster than the ships themselves, for crews often hailed each other and transferred mail and news at sea.

I was touched by the poignant story our guide told of Waving Girl Statue , which salutes Florence Martus, who is said to have greeted every ship that entered the Port of Savannah from 1887 to 1931.

Then our guide pointed to the sable palm and palmetto palm, state trees of South Carolina and Florida. I found it ironic that the symbolic trees of both states should flourish today in Georgia, which was established as a colony to provide a buffer between these English and Spanish territories.

Inside the Davenport House our guide pointed out the heart pine floors. As this wood ages, it grows harder. These floors now looked magnificent even though Davenport House had been restored after years of abuse as a tenement, subject to neglect and hard use.

We were shown an adjustable fire screen. I'd seen many of these in Europe and America but no one had explained their purpose before. Women's makeup used to contain beeswax, which melts easily. The fire screen shielded women's faces from the heat so their makeup would not melt. On the other hand, if the makeup became too cold and hard, a smile might cause it to crack. Hence the origin of the expression "to crack a smile," and perhaps, even an explanation of the enigma of Mona Lisa.

I next discovered something that my eight years of learning about wool and Tibetan rug weaving and spinning had never revealed: the wheel used to wind yarn as it was spun was called a "weasel." It had a counting device that popped every so many revolutions. "Pop goes the weasel," the familiar nursery song, came from what was once a common household occurrence.

For contrast, the bus next took us to the Telfair House, now the Telfair Academy of Arts & Sciences. Both Davenport House and Telfair were the homes of wealthy people. But Telfair, built later, is more formal in structure and design. The front is original; the rear has been extended to facilitate its role as a museum. The gallery had a fine George Bellows, called *Snow- Capped River,* painted in 1910. It reminded me of his *Men on the Docks,* which used to greet me each time I entered the Randolph-Macon Woman's College Library while I was a student. There were interesting Childe Hassim works and much too much to study in detail on a short visit. We finished our tour with visits to the oldest Methodist and Baptist churches and the oldest black churches in Georgia.

Having worked up a suitable appetite by early afternoon, I reclaimed my bicycle and rode it straight to Mrs. Wilkes' for lunch. Even without advertisements or Chamber of Commerce handouts, people seem to find her boarding house on Jones Street to enjoy her delicious, abundant food. The line to get in says it all. Inside, the walls are covered with articles from *Esquire, Savannah, People, Town & Country, Redbook, Time, Southern Living, Brown's Guide to Georgia,* and numerous newspapers, including the *Washington Post* and *Belgium Weekly Gazette.* I couldn't read the Chinese, Japanese, and Hindi publication names.

After sweet potatoes, greens, summer squash, barbecue, succotash with tomatoes, and biscuits, I couldn't resist her fried chicken, key lime pie, and gallons of sweet tea. I skipped the mashed potatoes and gravy, rice and gravy, butterbeans, beets, fried rice, and several other dishes.

Thus restored, fortified, and overfed, I pedaled in and out among the 22 half-acre park squares that dominate the design of Savannah. Laid out by founder James Edward Oglethorpe, each square has a story and a central monument or fountain. Live oaks fill many squares. Of the buildings surrounding them, public-use structures usually face east and west, while living quarters face north and south. Originally, the squares were common ground, where people could assemble during emergencies and livestock could graze at other times. Johnson, Reynolds, Wright, Madison, and Whitfield are squares of special interest.

I photographed 417 Congress Street — one of the few remaining saltbox houses in the earliest style, made of wood. Notable for their small size and design, many such houses were later expanded. They often burned and were replaced with brick structures.

I also managed to find the black dolphin downspout that I'd heard existed. The dolphin downspouts were designed by an apprentice at Bailey's Forge. About ten years ago, owner Ivan Bailey, a blacksmith trained in Germany, moved the forge from Savannah to Atlanta. Although they are not very old, the dolphin downspouts have the look of history and are Savannah originals. Few remain.

No matter how often I visit Savannah, there seem to be more places of historic and artistic merit. I had crammed the day full. When I returned to Courtney's home, several phone calls to friends answered their questions about bills, mail, and the rest of ordinary life and prepared me for further vagabonding.

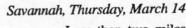

Savannah, Thursday, March 14

Downspout in Savannah

Less than two miles from Courtney's house, the rear tire went flat again! I had learned to let the bike rest on its panniers on one side and slide the wheel out without having to unload everything. Then, I sat down on a curb and took the time to carefully patch the tube. While the glue dried, I searched inside the tire. My fingers discovered a bit of glue or tar stuck inside the tire casing, the same thing that had caused the previous flat. It was a manufacturing defect I had not found the first time. At last, the tire was pumped up again and the bicycle reassembled.

Continuing south on Abercorn, which became GA 204, I turned onto US 17 South, and once again traveled the Atlantic Coastal Highway toward Richmond Hill. I had pedaled it with Courtney, and alone, on training rides out of Savannah. Going north during the USA perimeter tour about four years ago, I'd come this way. More recently, the Pedal for Power fund-raiser ride from Maine to Florida had used this road. Now I noted changes, more buildings and a general cleanup along the route. As

I had every other time I'd passed it, I vowed to return to one particularly cluttered antique shop. Today I could carry nothing more.

The US 17 road shoulder was fine, but I turned right on Canebreak Road, then immediately left on Basin Road for a short, quiet stretch between US 17 and I-95. Here, the lily pads growing in the swamp, Spanish moss swaying from trees, and yellow jasmine climbing over everything like honeysuckle were more noticeable than traffic. It was curious to ride this stretch through the trees, so quiet and isolated, yet still within earshot of both major highways. Heavy trucks and speeding cars weren't really present — just ghostly sounds — until I reentered US 17 at Kings Ferry Park, crossed the bridge, left Chatham County, and entered Bryan County.

At the Richmond Hill Food Lion, I bought yogurt and salad makings, then continued through the rest of the highway interchanges, noting Jiffy Foods, Flash Foods, and Express Foods, all designed for gas-and-go travelers. Later in the day I passed a Fast Lane Mini-Mart.

Continuing on US 17, I arrived at Midway Museum and found Kathy McNamara, a reporter for the *Coastal Courier* in Hinesville, interviewing Joann Clark, the museum's custodian. Joann asked if I would like to look at the kitchen and Midway Church before she guided me through the museum. She handed me a very large key to the church, whose congregation had always been characterized by patriotism, public service, and industry. Its founders, in 1754, set a tone that resulted in outstanding leadership for Georgia and for our country. Standing in the center aisle of the restored old building, I heard no sound but the whispers of history.

The Midway region of Liberty County was settled about 1752 by Puritans and Huguenots who came from South Carolina, seeking new lands to settle. At that time, Georgia, like Louisiana, still called its counties parishes. In what is now Liberty County, a militia troop was organized in 1788 that is still active today. The region prospered economically as residents worked hard to build our country. During the Civil War, under Kilpatrick, Sherman's troops used the fine, high brick wall of the Midway cemetery to hold confiscated livestock. The union troops destroyed the rail line near the Altamaha River and devastated the plantations to such an extent that Liberty County's economy has never regained the importance it held in early Georgia's political, economic, and military life.

I walked back under the largest live oaks I'd ever seen, and discovered that Kathy was getting ready to drive to Sunbury for another interview.

Sunbury was ten miles away and I had never been there. Since there was only one road to Sunbury, she would have to return this way, so I asked if I could ride along in the car and look at the historic site while she did her interview. She seemed glad to take me. I ate my lunch while waiting for her, excited that I would get to visit Sunbury State Historic Site, including Fort Morris/Fort Defiance. I left my bicycle behind the Midway Museum.

During the drive to Sunbury, Kathy told me that Hinesville, further inland, has a larger population than Brunswick and is situated right outside the gates of Fort Stewart. Kathy likes the coastal area better than Atlanta. She feels that individuality is more acceptable there than in a big city, and coastal people judge each other by character rather than externals such as money and clothes.

"Up there, the good-looking people marry the good-looking people and that's how it goes," she said. "Here along the coast, personality and what people do for the community seem to have more importance than appearance and material assets. I appreciate life and feel more comfortable in a small town where individuality is more of an asset than a liability."

Kathy also shared some of the history of Sunbury as we traveled. Situated on a bluff, twenty-seven feet high and seven miles inland, it was once an important port city. Savannah, on the other hand, is on a forty-foot bluff, and seventeen miles inland. In 1773, Sunbury handled 56 ships, a third as many as Savannah's 160. In 1775, there were 1,000 people living in Sunbury. It was home to two signers of the Declaration of Independence. During the Revolutionary War, three American invasions of British-held East Florida were launched from Sunbury. Later, when the British demanded surrender of Fort Morris, the defenders shouted in defiant tones, "Come and take it!" — which the British did in 1779. Later, durring the war of 1812, a rebuilt, smaller fort was named Defiance, in remembrance of that act of courage. But today, Sunbury is a dead town, the victim of economic, not military, ills. Kathy's knowledge of the background of early structures made it a much more interesting excursion than I had expected.

During our return to Midway, Kathy told me about her adventures in Saudi Arabia, as a member of the press, during Operation Desert Storm. She had lived in the tents with the soldiers and felt she learned about their lives.

The first time she met a Saudi, she asked him to explain why their religion requires prayer so many times a day in a public fashion. He explained the customs to her and told her she was the first American he had met who asked any questions about Saudi culture, manners, or religion. He was pleased that she wanted to learn about them. It turned out that he was the Saudi Minister of Information, and he helped arrange an extension of her stay. She got an article published in the Atlanta paper, as well as several local articles. A good start on her first career job.

Back in Midway, named presumably because of its location between Savannah and Darien, my thoughts were drawn to Revolutionary times. Liberty County and the Midway area provided me with an understanding of colonial coastal Georgia I'd found nowhere else. In the cemetery, I found the Roswell King family plot. He had migrated inland and founded Roswell, near Atlanta. On some stones I found names common in my mother's family, such as McCullough.

I pedaled south toward Darien on the Dixie Highway, or US 17. It was built and paved in the late 1920s and 1930s and follows its unpaved ancestor, the Post Road, hacked out from Savannah to Darien by Oglethorpe's men, with the help of Indian guides. My thoughts moved back in history to antebellum rice and cotton plantations of the Altamaha delta, land populated by the French in the 1750, while the Spanish and English vied with the Indians and each other over its possession.

It took me longer than anticipated to reach Darien, for a headwind blew steadily all afternoon. I heard frogs in the water along the road. I stopped for a refreshment break at the Jiffy Food in Eulonia, just as four boys came out with cold drinks in their hands. We talked for a bit. Students from Gainesville, on spring break, they had bicycled from Orlando. Two of the boys had pedaled across America on their own last summer; the other two were on their first self-contained tour. They camped anywhere and slept late, gaining weight and having a good time. They couldn't afford campgrounds and were carrying about half what I was. Even though they were only traveling a week and had no changes for their tattered T-shirts, they were effusive about the freedom on the road. Friends would meet them in Savannah and drive them and their bicycles back in time for the start of classes. I hesitatingly admitted to myself that I envied their light loads, their pedaling with the wind, and their jolly company. Today they had eaten at Archie's, in Darien, and had come up GA 99 past Ridgeville's lovely homes, as I had done in previous years. With the headwind, I decided to stay on shorter, but parallel, US 17.

In Darien, I turned onto GA 251 and came to rest a mile and a half later, at Inland Harbor Campground, where I was welcomed by Betty Ansink, who told me which site to use. She was taking hot rolls out of the oven and I bought half a dozen for supper. While I was pitching my tent, a wild swamp sow and two of her half-grown piglets trotted over to welcome me, too. There was never any trouble disposing of apple cores during my two-day stay there!

I telephoned Carolyn Hodges, owner-manager of the Open Gates Bed & Breakfast on Vernon Square, and arranged to stay there Saturday and join her tour to Sapelo Island. Sapelo Island is not accessible to tourists every day. I was determined to go there again and see more of the island than the half-day regular tour permitted. But for now, I was happy to rest in my tent.

Darien, Inland Harbor Campground, Friday, March 15

I slept well but awakened with cold feet. The nights were still chilly for camping out. A lazy morning of showering, then reading in my tent came to an end when my stomach told me it was time for breakfast. I'd eaten all available fruit. It was warm enough to wear shorts and a cotton shirt for the first time! On the way to Archie's Restaurant, I stopped to reread an historical marker about the River Road:

The river road has changed little in location since its beginning as a military route in 1739. Scottish Highlanders first marched over it on their way to invade Spanish Florida, and troops have used it in three wars: the war with Spain, the Revolutionary War, and the War between the States. As a civilian highway, this road inland first served as the road between Fort Barrington and a ferry. Later it was the important link in the old Macon to Darien Highway used by planters for their carriages, stage-coaches, and horseback riders carrying mail or traveling during the early 19th century. Fort Barrington, 12 miles west on the Altamaha River, was built in 1751. Called Fort Howe during the Revolution, it guarded the most dangerous land pass on the southern frontier of Georgia.

I intended to take GA 251 to see the fort, but never had time. I wouldn't mind returning to Darien — I feel so comfortable there. Every time I visit, it occurs to me that I could have lived there in some other time, as an Indian, Highlander, logger, or sailor. I believe every individual experiences multiple incarnations, whether they know it or acknowledge it or not. I also feel sure that our amnesia about past lives is necessary to keep us looking ahead. Imagine how the study of history and genealogy would blur the present had we better hindsight! And yet, a momentary sense of prescience or recollection about people and places, adverse or comfortable, can be instructive. The whole notion is motivating, for if I am now reaping what I have sown and will in future reap what I have earned, shouldn't I make every effort to do what is right?

At Archie's Restaurant, I was greeted by Archie himself. "You remember meeting Talbot Harding, don't you?" he asked, indicating a gentleman rising from his chair. We shook hands, and Talbot invited me to sit down at a table with him and several others. I ordered coffee and breakfast. Mr. Harding told me his son had been stationed in Washington and was now posted elsewhere since we had met here about four years ago. It is always pleasant to be remembered. He suggested I phone the owner of Ashantilly (a winter home built in 1820 by Thomas Spalding of Sapelo Island) so that I could meet him and see the house. He warned me that Mr. Haynes was quite hard of hearing, and I should not be offended if he did not invite me there. Mr. Haynes operates the nationally known Ashantilly Press on the grounds, printing handset type on special papers of interest and value. Although I phoned several times, I was unable to reach him and had to add him to the "next time" list.

On the edge of Darien, I visited Fort King George State Historic Site, where, on a high spot overlooking the marsh, a blockhouse from the southern outpost of the British Empire in North America has been reconstructed. The original structure was built between 1721 and 1732. I climbed all over the blockhouse and walked the surrounding area, impressed by its small size and important mission. It was the first fortification to counteract French and Spanish expansion and the first English settlement on land that is now Georgia.

The cypress blockhouse and palisaded, earthen fort were occupied for seven years by British soldiers from His Majesty's 41st Independent Company. They endured incredible hardships and disease resulting from the harsh coastal conditions. Two-thirds of the British troops stationed there died, and for nine years only two lookouts remained.

At the slide show and exhibits, I learned that the earliest known inhabitants of coastal Georgia were Creek Indians of Muskogean stock. The Spanish name for the Creeks was Guale. It might be interesting to look further into the meaning, origin, and use of that word along the coast. Today, it describes a spoken dialect. The Guale Indians used dugout canoes, drank a tea-like drink, and played games that trained them in skills for hunting.

The slide show also illustrated the worldwide importance of the vast marsh delta of the Altamaha, the longest river in Georgia. Spanish claims to Georgia territory occurred from 1500 and into the early 1700s. After the Spanish priests established missions (as they did in California), the Indians became dependent on the Europeans until, in 1597, they rebelled and killed a priest. The area was then left uninhabited by Europeans for a time. French involvement in the area apparently began about 1702 with a new frontier policy to stretch east from Louisiana and encircle the British. The French took Pensacola, erected Fort Toulouse in Alabama in 1717, and then began scouting east along the Altamaha River, from its source toward the Atlantic Ocean.

It's no small wonder the English felt the need of a buffer zone between their dozen colonies and the French and Spanish claims along the Mississippi River and in Florida. British troops from Darien participated in the battle of Bloody Marsh near Fort Frederica, ending Spanish aggression in the area. Through agreement between England and Spain in 1739, the north side of the St. Marys River, east to its source and west to the Mississippi River, or perhaps to the Pacific Ocean, became Georgia's southern border. Darien became the new southern frontier for the English.

After the fort was abandoned, General James Oglethorpe brought a group of Scottish Highlanders to the area in 1736, three years after the founding of Savannah, and settled them upstream on a bluff in Darien. A sawmilling boom led Darien to boast of being one of the world's largest timber exporters. Lumber was exported until 1925. The foundations of several early sawmills are still visible.

Before leaving home, I had begun to read *Early Days on the Georgia Tidewater: The Story of McIntosh County & Sapelo,* written by Buddy Sullivan and published by the *Darien News* in 1990. While riding around town, I saw the office and entered to meet and thank Buddy for producing such a comprehensive work.

In Savannah, I had learned that Oglethorpe permitted neither slaves nor lawyers among the first settlers. Indentured servants were allowed but there were not enough of them to clear and cultivate the land. Many landowners wanted to have slaves, as in Carolina, because their crops were so labor intensive.

People unable to adapt to colonial life were complainers, labeled "clamorous malcontents." In his book Sullivan quotes from the *Colonial Records of Georgia* of 1739, regarding a report about eighteen of the Scottish settlers at Darien who petitioned against the importation of slaves. It has been termed the first recorded protest against slavery in America. The Scots' petition said, in part: "Introduce slaves and we cannot but believe they will one day return to be a scourge and a curse upon our children and children's children." Their values did not win out, nor did their descendents endure in large numbers.

I continued a quiet pedal tour of Darien, the second-oldest planned town in Georgia. Though much smaller than Savannah, Darien was also laid out in squares, several of which remain as parks. The town had the good fortune to experience two economic "boom" eras in the 19th century, although its population never exceeded 2,000 permanent residents. I wondered whether that count included full-time plantation residents or only landholders who had town houses. It did omit people who owned no land. Butler Island and the Hofwyl-Broadfield Plantations I had visited previously, and they remained on my "come back" list, while a ceremonial "Blessing of the Fleet" of shrimp boats and the reenactment at Fort King George hold places on the "next time" list.

McIntosh County continues to be one of the poorest counties in Georgia. It is also, in my view, among Georgia's historical treasure troves. Botanist William Bartram traveled the coastal wilderness from 1773 to 1777, visiting many of the same places that I have. Over 800 historical sites in Darien, and in the county, have been identified for preservation in the next twenty years. I'm glad to have visited the area before the tourist boom occurs.

After confirming with Carolyn Hodges that I would be at Open Gates Bed & Breakfast early in the morning for the tour of Sapelo, I returned to camp and leisure. The afternoon had turned cold, and I realized it was still too soon to mail away long cycling pants and sweaters. Spring flowers may have come out, but the warmer temperatures weren't yet stable.

Betty Ansink was baking zucchini bread. I bought a loaf for supper, as well as a dozen of her delicious rolls. Lunch at Archie's had satisfied me, so I decided to make supper out of what I was carrying, supplemented by Betty's fresh baked goods. Tomorrow, I would visit Sapelo in Carolyn Hodges' compact motor boat, spend the night at the Open Gates Bed & Breakfast, then pedal to Brunswick on Sunday morning for sightseeing and a visit with my friend Lori, who lived there. I planned to spend Sunday night in a motel on St. Simons Island at Epworth-by-the-Sea, to allow me time on Monday to explore Sea Island, St. Simons, and Brunswick, before pedaling south to St. Marys.

When Betty heard my travel plans, she told me she would be going to St. Simons Island the next day to visit her daughter and could carry my panniers there. Delighted, I repacked overnight gear into two smaller containers and arranged to put tent, sleeping bag, and two panniers in Betty's station wagon before I left in the morning.

Darien, Inland Harbor Campground, Saturday, March 16

Betty and her husband John, a retired marine, had come to run the campground because their children lived nearby and they liked the area. As we were stowing my gear in her car, she told me that Darien was burned in 1863 by black soldiers among Sherman's troops. They came from the north or were recruited in South Carolina. The movie *Glory* records this event. Everyone had left Darien except for a few old people. The women and children had gone to the Ridge (Ridgeville) and the men were away in the war. Bars and prostitutes accompanied the logging boom that followed, but since 1864 the economy had been depressed. It is getting better now.

Betty told me about her home. "This is a little town on the water. People are ole timers, independent, they had to be to survive here. They like it and don't like people who try to change anything. Change is coming, though. In the past two years a house on the water, a modern condo, has doubled in value. There's a lot of history around here.

"Eugenia Price is writing a new book on Ebo Landing and she plans to do one on Darien soon," Betty said she'd heard. "Price lives near where her children do on St. Simons Island. Read the Fanny Kemble book *Journal of a Residence on a Georgian Plantation;* it is really good. No one around here will read it, but it is interesting." (I did read the former English actress' book later, and Betty was right. It contains interesting details of life on the Butler plantation during the winter of 1838-39.)

It interests me how people spend their retirement. I would think running a campground is an awful lot of work, but it is also seasonal. Betty told me that spring and fall are the major seasons here along I-95, for people driving to and from Florida, but there is some business in summer too. John works four days at a golf course as a security guard, which I hope is a sit-down job. Here he does all the heavy work: cutting the grass, cleaning the bathhouses, helping people with repairs, or answering questions. Betty collects fees, directs people to sites, bakes, and cooks jellies. She's always busy doing something, but never too busy to chat.

I had to get going, so ate a quick breakfast of pancakes at Archie's, then rolled into the backyard at Open Gates a little after 9 A.M., ready for the boat trip to Sapelo Island. Andy and Cindy, who were going too, met me and told me Carolyn would be out soon. We got acquainted while hitching the boat trailer to Carolyn's car.

Carolyn joined us. We discovered that all of us had experience sailing small boats. Carolyn had sailed a Flying Dutchman on Lake Allatoona near Atlanta, where she had sailed in the same fleet as Ted Turner. I had raced on the Chesapeake Bay; Andy and Cindy had sailed near where they grew up. We identified mutual friends, and Carolyn's patter about McIntosh County punctuated our journey. She told us that the large number of airstrips in the county contributed to the heaviest drug trade in the region and made it hard to control, but deterrence was working now. Halting her car at Blue's Hall Dock, she introduced us to Italeen Stewart, whose husband had died and left her to carry on the boat launching business alone.

Our day was overcast. Wind blew white caps into the tidal river water, despite the shelter of offshore islands. A couple of chaps in a larger fishing boat told Carolyn they'd keep a weather eye out for us as we crossed Doboy Sound, which cut through miles of marsh grass to reach Sapelo Island. She laughed and asked if we would like a bit of adventure or if we minded getting wet. I felt comfortable observing her careful attention to tide, wind, and safety. Carolyn was an experienced sailor.

I was wearing the wool bicycling hat that I'd worn daily under my helmet. I had on two wool sweaters and my rain jacket of lined Gortex, but was still chilly. Cindy Davis said she was also cold. Andy Harthcock seemed better dressed for the weather than his wife or myself.

Carolyn talked and rushed about enough to keep us entertained and herself warm while she deftly launched the boat. We launched at high tide, about 10:00 A.M., and would return at low tide, about 4:00 P.M. Carolyn was a good boat driver so I had no fears and listened as she pointed out the various islands, trees, creeks, and rivers of the marsh. We bounced over rolling swells in her small outboard with cutty and windshield. Though it was cold, laughter warmed us, and she certified us as "happy campers." It was good to be on the water again. I realized how much I missed sailing and racing small sailboats, which had so consumed my free time in the 1960s.

At the Sapelo dock, we located the old car Carolyn had rented. We found the keys under the seat and transferred our gear from the boat before slowly bumping over the sandy roads to see the R. J. Reynolds home. A tour bus was there, so we drove around and waited until they departed. Carolyn took us into the kitchen and introduced us to the people working there. They were selling handmade wreaths, baskets, and other sweet-grass products. Their prices were low because we were buying directly from them instead of a shop.

One of these islanders had provided the car and another had brought a bicycle for me, so I could pedal around Sapelo Island as part of my perimeter tour. I rode it for photographs, but I didn't want to ride anywhere else while the others traveled by car, for I would miss the chatter and laughter. Alone on the road, it doesn't take long to hunger for company.

At the nearby pond, we saw an ibis, a red-faced common moorhen, and a deer.

While the tourists climbed back into their bus, Carolyn explained the architecture of the R. J. Reynolds house. Its building material, tabby, is made by mixing equal parts slaked lime (from cooking ancient desalted oyster shells), sand, water, and shells. There are no rocks or building stone on the Georgia seacoast. Tabby was to colonials what cement is to us. It was mixed and placed in forms to harden, then layered until a wall was complete.

Settlements of Europeans on Sapelo date from the early 1500s. We didn't see many people today; most of the Hog Hammock Community had departed to attend a wedding elsewhere.

We were impressed by Thomas Spalding's estate, as later expanded by R. J. Reynolds. There were huge greenhouses that we thought should be used for something. The University of Georgia occupies some buildings for marine research. Several of the small cottages, ordered long ago from Sears and Roebuck and occupied by university people, had been well maintained.

President Jimmy Carter and his wife stayed at the Reynolds estate during holidays several times while he was president, and we saw the airstrip where they landed. A group of birdwatchers was spending the weekend in the estate mansion. Any nonprofit group can rent it for an educational outing, but weekends are booked over a year in advance, so a midweek event would be easier to arrange.

We drove the full length of the island, looked across at Blackbeard Island, tramped around in several ruined buildings, and ate our picnic lunch in the protection of a local hunting camp. The owner wasn't there, but we turned on the radio, and sat in the chairs while eating.

All too soon, we returned to our boat and had a quieter, drier trip back while Carolyn pointed out islands that had been created out of ballast stones, dumped in selected spots by sailing ships. Trees and plants were growing on the islands. Some even had cabins. Joe Jurskis runs the Blackbeard Sailing School nearby, an intensive, hands-on class using Rhodes 19 boats.

On our way home, I was shocked that two of the best and oldest homes at the Ridge had been moved away and burned, leaving old beautiful trees shading empty holes, surrounded by ancient fences.

At Open Gates, I was shown my room, cleaned up and rested. Rain began to stream down. The weather prediction was for thundershowers that night and hard, steady rain all the next day. I debated what to do.

Before dinner, we chatted with the other Open Gates guests. They were two couples, from Florida and North Carolina, who met in Darien for the weekend because of its central location. Then we Sapelo veterans climbed back into the car with Carolyn. She drove us to Shellman Bluff, a fishing camp north of Eulonia, where we ate a fresh broiled flounder dinner at Hunter's Cafe caught that morning by proprietor Britt Altman. I dozed in the car going home and fell asleep as soon as my head hit the pillow on my bed.

Darien, Open Gates Bed & Breakfast, Sunday, March 17

Dressed in handsome garb, Carolyn served her guests Plantation Pancakes and a compote of fresh fruit. When questioned, she admitted they were called Hawaiian pancakes in a *New York Times Cookbook* recipe. We ate them with gallberry honey or mayhaw jelly. After breakfast, we had more coffee and Irish fortune cookies, a gift of international guests. They tasted like Chinese fortune cookies, but the sayings inside gave them away:

"The older the fiddle, the sweeter the tune. Irish proverb."

"Baloney is flattery so thick it cannot be true; blarney is flattery so thin we like it. Irish saying."

"Depend on the rabbit's foot if you will—but remember, it didn't work for the rabbit. R. E. Shay."

Everyone else had plans for the day. Carolyn urged I stay over another night, for Monday was to be clear and sunny. With a cold rain falling steadily, she didn't have to insist. I spent most of the day in her library, quietly reading about Georgia, glad to be alone.

One article was entitled, "Hair Today, Shorn Tomorrow," about hair artwork. Carolyn has a fine, framed example of it, dated 1881. Her great grandmother had constructed the floral still life using different colors of hair provided by her dearest friends. I had to look closely to realize it was hair art for it looked a bit like lace in detail. To make such handcraft one needs human hair; annealed wire, floss, thread, or cord for wrapping; gold, cut steel, or glass beads for centers; scissors; knitting needles in two or three sizes; and, I would add, deft fingers and enormous patience.

Late Sunday afternoon it was still raining. Carolyn and I met Andy and Cindy at the Two Way Fish Camp, run by Bill and Chip Croft. A license is required for fresh-water, but not for salt-water fishing. Two Way Fish Camp is a marina under the fourth bridge south of Darien, located where the tide changes. Upstream is freshwater; downstream is salt water. Unfortunately, it was too early to see the West Indian manatee. They return from Florida in May and swim in these waters through October, eating as much as 100 pounds of vegetation per day. Their primary food is the smooth cordgrass, the dominant plant in coastal salt marshes. Sometimes called sea cows, manatees are warm-blooded, air-breathing creatures of placid expression and calm disposition.

We ate some of the best barbecue sandwiches I'd ever had. Andy and Cindy departed for their home near Macon. Carolyn and I returned to Open Gates. It was still raining as we drove back across the Altamaha Delta, over the South Altamaha River, Champney River, Butler River, and Darien River. Carolyn drove me around the former Butler (rice) Plantation, and we were fortunate enough to see an enormous flock of glossy ibis while she explained the buildings, fields, and places along the river that Fanny Kemble mentioned in her book. I spent the rest of the evening in Carolyn's library or reading in bed.

Darien, Open Gates B&B, Monday, March 18

At breakfast I was introduced, as were we all, to mayhaws. They are called berries, but technically haws are in the apple family. The tart red fruit grows in the swamps and bogs of southwest Georgia near Colquitt in Miller County. The trees grow wild in that small area, and the berries are prized for the delicate-flavored, sweet jelly they make.

Talk swirled around children's stories, specifically *The Country Bunny* and the *Little Gold Shoes* by DuBose Heyward. Carolyn showed us these from her collection of antique children's books, and read a few scenes aloud while we were gathered around her table during breakfast. I enjoyed the camaraderie of the Florida and North Carolina people. I also appreciated the company of John Schafer, whom we had met on the dock the day before. He appeared and disappeared in the

kitchen or dining room, assisting as an informal host while Carolyn's husband was out of town. John was a quiet man with the talents of a mechanical wizard and excellent sailing skills.

Rain had changed to mist as I pedaled away from Darien, without having been able to revisit the Hofwyl-Broadfield Plantation (closed on Monday), where rice was last grown commercially in Georgia. As I pedaled over the four delta bridges and south, my ears were ringing with fellowship, laughter, and the cheer of a delightful weekend.

As I approached Brunswick at midmorning, the rain stopped, the sun came out, and I smiled at the sign "Dog and Cattery Country Club." I continued over the bridge to Epworth-by-the-Sea, ate lunch, and registered for a room. There was some trouble finding my panniers because the person I asked said, "We put all baggage being held here and if it isn't here we don't have it." I wandered about and looked in corners and soon found it behind a sales counter.

After finding and stashing my luggage in a room overlooking the river, I pedaled out Sea Island Road and Frederica Road, visited Christ Church, then continued to Fort Frederica. I watched the slide show and walked through the restored town on a sunny, pleasant afternoon. In addition to historic ruins, there were quite a few red-bellied woodpeckers. On the way back, I pedaled Sea Island Drive, then returned toward St. Simons town, and just reached the Retreat Avenue junction when the front tire went flat. I was carrying nothing, not even my pump, although I did have a spare tube. I got off the bicycle and stood on the corner at the junction, looking around. What should I do now? I was only about two miles from Epworth but didn't want to walk, rolling the bike. Then I saw it — a bike shop — and headed straight there! Benji's Bike Shop soon had me rolling again, both tires pumped up to full pressure. (I seldom do that with the hand pump.) I reached Epworth in time for supper.

Steve Vose came to visit. He was a local man who'd sent me directions for bicycling the area and who had just returned from Dublin's annual St. Patrick's Century Ride (where he'd ridden fifty miles in the pouring rain). We expressed mutual regret that we hadn't yet been able to ride together. While Steve and I were comparing bicycle rides we'd enjoyed and identifying a few mutual friends, Lori Morgan Pirkle arrived with her wedding album under her arm. We had missed connections for lunch so she came to visit. Lori had also participated in the bicycle ride from north Georgia to Savannah that traced Sherman's march, so she didn't mind our bicycle talk.

After Steve left, I was able to enjoy the photos and hear details of Lori's wedding. I thought she and her new husband were smart not to spend all of their savings to get married. They were wed in the bandstand by the St. Simon's Lighthouse; the reception was a picnic in the nearby park. Their day was sunny and the pictures were wonderful. There could have been no improvement on the setting.

I was glad to see Steve and Lori and appreciated their visits. But rearranging because of yesterday's rain, trying to schedule visits with friends, pedaling a whole day, and making notes had exhausted me. I doubt Lori's car engine had whirred into action before I was asleep.

St. Simons Island, Epworth-by-the-Sea, Tuesday, March 19

Determined not to leave without seeing the town of St. Simon's, I pedaled past the airport to the pier, wondering if I would recognize any place from early childhood visits. We had stayed in a large wooden boarding house with a wrap-around porch, overlooking the ocean. I found houses of that era back from the beach, but on the beach itself everything had been rebuilt, and porches were replaced with decks. Back under the trees I could almost remember how it felt fifty-plus years ago.

I mailed off a package of warm clothes, but kept one sweater and some emergency clothes in case the balmy weather wasn't here to stay. Then I visited the lighthouse and museum and met the new curator, Elizabeth Furlow, for a long discussion about her job and her excitement at working there.

She was interested in my reactions to St. Simons and my attempts to find places recognizable to a faint, 50-year-old memory. Her grandmother, younger than I, was also coming back for a visit — I don't consider myself grandmotherly.

I returned to Epworth for lunch, then packed up my gear. My departure was delayed by a conversation with a painter who has lived on the island for 34 years. He loves it but has a place in Brevard and likes to go to the mountains, too.

Finally underway, I pedaled over the bridge and causeway bicycle path. When pedaling up a bridge, it is well to notice the expansion joints — the size and how they are made — so that you will know what to expect while speeding down the other side. Here, I also noticed newly planted oleander and palm trees along the route; they should look fine in a few years. The marsh was still tan with occasional greening patches.

I was once again on a stretch of road familiar from the Pedal for Power. As a group, we usually rode in a paceline, or talking, certainly paying more attention to our companions than the scenery, which is mostly trees anyway. I especially liked this part of the Pedal for Power ride because it is flat and the road's so smooth. It provides a wonderful opportunity to practice paceline techniques. Traffic is light, too. Even with maximum concentration on what you are doing, you don't miss much, except another pine forest on both sides.

This time, I noted that mailboxes are in the normal place along the road, but they face away from the highway. The mail car drove on the grassy shoulder so it wasn't necessary to reach across the passenger seat to insert mail into the boxes. I'd never seen that done before.

Woodbine was ten miles ahead and Kingsland was twenty-two. I passed the time eating Nutri/System Craving Control Snack —sweet tarts that take a long time to melt and can't be chewed. Monday's 54 miles were easy, but half of those were with an unloaded bike and the rest with half a load. Now, after about 40 miles, I was tired. It was warm and humid. The route looked just as it did on the perimeter tour four years ago. Maybe some day I will take a turn off the highway, through

Woodbine, but I was not going an extra inch now. It was almost 5:00 P.M., and I had to arrive somewhere before dark. I wanted to reach Crooked River State Park, but getting there before dark would be difficult.

"Appropriate that Woodbine should have a crawfish festival," I thought as I pedaled along, "because it seems so like Louisiana, with swamp water on both sides. Whoops! Stop." I got off my bike and pulled out the camera for pictures of an old cane mill at about the 12-mile post between Woodbine and Kingsland. It was on the grass between two houses. My presence stirred up all the neighborhood dogs but none came running before I was underway again. There were lots of cypress and pine on both sides of the road with plenty of moss.

I reminded myself to shake my head from side to side and back and forth, to loosen up my spine, and to shake out my shoulders, to prevent tension and fatigue. I have to remember to keep my spine flexible and not in one position too long.

I passed an historical marker for the Post Road to St. Marys; it looked like I could shortcut that way, but it wasn't on my map. I stopped at a service station and the man said I could go that way, but it would be at the risk of getting lost, and wouldn't save a lot of time. He said Crooked River State Park was about 15 miles ahead and the KOA near Kingsland was even closer.

But that wouldn't do. Kingsland would be further in the morning; I'd surely have go-to-work traffic and might be late getting to the boat for Cumberland Island. I told myself, "I've got to get to the state park. It is reputed to be a nice park and I've wanted to go there for years. Today is the day."

Soon I came to Harriett's Bluff Road. "If I could get to the state park from the Post Road, I can from here, too."

I turned left. A few miles later, I rode over I-95 and to a Jiffy Food store. The lady explained that I must return over the interstate, take the first and second left, make a third left at a four-lane road, and then another at the entrance to the sub base. I began to realize I would not get there before sunset, but maybe I'd make it by twilight. I turned left on Old Still Road and pedaled as hard as I could — surprised at how well I could move the load when I put some determination into it.

"Why did I put my emergency blinker tail light down in the bottom of a pannier? No time to get it out now — the frogs are talking in the ditches."

I kept pedaling, and reached Crooked River State Park in mid-twilight. By the time I found a site, mosquitoes were chewing ferociously on the backs of my legs and on my ears. It was almost black when I found the flashlight and Skin-So-Soft. I had to use the flashlight to hammer in the last tent pegs. I threw everything into the tent except what I needed for a shower. When I ran the water and put my hand in, it was warm; when I stepped in, it turned cold, and set me shivering. I forgot my towel, so I dried off with my neck scarf. I put on a shirt, sweatshirt, and sweatpants. Then I washed my riding shorts in the basin while the girl next to me combed her wet, cold hair. Cindy and her friends had just come in from three days of canoeing in the swamp. She was glad for the bath at any temperature. I recalled the fine time we had had swamp canoeing years ago, when I had looked at the town of St. Marys and found every house for sale, cheap. Now they are sought after and expensive.

I asked Cindy about the Millersville sweatshirt she wore. She told me 15 students were on spring break from Millersville University in Pennsylvania. I had attended a League of American Wheelmen bicycle rally there one summer. We talked about riding bikes in the area, where there are only Amish buggies to contend with while "doing" the short, frequently steep hills.

Cindy and her friend Andy came over to my tent and we continued talking until the park ranger stopped in his pickup. He told me I'd taken a reserved site, and would have to move or pay extra. I would have to move anyway, if the person who reserved it came in the night. I excused myself from our chat and wandered around with the flashlight, looking for a site with no reserved sign on the stake. The ranger told me to take the next site but I thought a mobile home was on it. A lady was standing in its doorway. I said hello and asked the site number. She and her husband asked me in for a cup of tea, then invited me to join them on the site, which I did, paying them half the fee. I was angry at the ranger, although he was only doing his job. We both knew it was unlikely anyone would come after the gate was locked at dark, but technically he was right. Park policy is often unfair to bicyclists.

I was glad for the opportunity to share and only pay half the fee. Moving the tent hadn't been as bad as I expected. It was freestanding, so I unstaked and emptied it but did not have to take it down. I carried it to the new place and put the stakes in again, then carried all the bundles and bits and pieces, hoping I didn't drop anything in the dark. Early the next morning, I walked over for a ground check to be sure. Actually, it was better to be in the shadow of the mobile home, because the campground lights wouldn't keep me awake.

By 8:30 P.M., I was finally moved and settled. I began to eat supper: a tin of beef pate (my last—Nutri/System had discontinued it), rye triskets, fresh mushrooms stuffed with pate, two of Betty's Ansink's homemade rolls, and water.

Then I called on my neighbors. Ernest and Ruth Limbach were most cordial. From Ohio, they were on their way to a Good Sam Club RV (recreation vehicle) rally in Florida, and were visiting friends and family along the way. Unfortunately, I could only remember a few names of the small towns in Ohio near Niles, where we visited last summer during the Pedal for Power Across America tour from Los Angeles to Boston. Ohio was one place we had gotten off the main highways and zigzagged the back roads, an interesting and pleasant ride that contrasted with the old, pre-interstate highways we often traveled.

I returned to my tent and bed about 10:00 P.M. It felt wonderful to lie down flat and stretch my spine. I had covered 67 miles — the last hour at a sort of sprint — but there were no aches or pains in my muscles. Training is wonderful.

Crooked River State Park, Wednesday, March 20

I usually awaken early, and never use a clock, because I don't like to hear the alarm ring. I have done this since I was a teen, and learned that I could "set my head" to awaken me at a certain time by thinking about it before going to sleep. For years, I would set a clock anyway, but there was a quiet tick or click in the clock before the alarm went off, and I always awoke fast enough to shut it off before that awful racket. Finally, I quit setting an alarm, and usually use no clock at all; I don't like the ticking. If I have to catch an airplane in the middle of the night, or something like that, I might use a backup. Recently, I've bought semi-waterproof dollar watches. I throw them away when they quit working. The cheaper types have bigger numbers that I can see with any combination of glasses I wear.

I awoke with the sun in the morning and sped to the town of St. Marys. I reached the office in time to take the 9:00 A.M. boat. I was hungry, though, and wouldn't get to see any of the town if I spent the whole day on Cumberland Island, so I registered for the 11:45 boat. It was a lovely, sunny day. I shot all my film and bought another roll. I talked with Glenn Smith at the Bookshop, had breakfast, and visited the houses and the museum in St. Marys, all worthwhile.

Glenn Smith had a deck prism for sale. It was a hand-poured reproduction from the *Charles W. Morgan* in Mystic. How had I missed that? They were used on wooden sailing ships because they would admit and refract light below decks, where the only light came through portholes. Candles and lanterns posed too great a fire danger on a wooden ship, especially in rough weather when the portholes were closed. Glenn thought it would be fine to build a house and insert these in the ceiling of a living or dining room.

I picked up the carry-out lunch I'd ordered and boarded the boat for Cumberland Island. On board, I asked a girl wearing a Randolph-Macon Woman's College sweatshirt if she attended there. She and two friends were on spring break. We talked about college and Lynchburg and what they had done for vacation and what I was doing. Nancy Lassig, sitting near us, was swept into the conversation, and invited me to call her and visit anytime I was in Atlanta. Max Maury, from Vidalia, couldn't resist our jabber about bicycling. He said he was in charge of arranging the BRAG stopover in Vidalia this June. We talked about the food bikers like, and he asked a lot of questions about how it is out on the road during the Bicycle Ride Across Georgia. Before we knew it, we were clambering off the boat onto Cumberland Island.

In the boat, we had been huddled groups; released to the Cumberland wilderness, we expanded in all directions. Carrying a water bottle, camera, and my styrofoam lunch packet, I sauntered under the live oaks along a sand track. The forest was quiet. Sun penetrated the shade like a million tiny spotlights, illuminating the leaves in more shades of green than I could count.

I looked in the small museum along the shore, then walked toward the ruins of Dungeness, Andrew and Lucy Carnegie's 1886 home and gardens. Some people were sitting at picnic tables under the live oaks, eating; others, like me, continued to walk. I entered the gates to the former mansion. The ruins were four or five stories high, and as long as a city block. The quiet was broken only by the occasional cry of a bird or a child. We all seemed to wander like awestruck ghosts of ourselves. Nature subdued us as it had the ruin. On the other side of the house, the clipped lawn held a sunken fountain. I was hungry, so after taking a few photos, I sat down on the edge of the fountain with my feet inside, where water should have been. I was facing the ruined Carnegie home. It reminded me of a novel I had read, *Elephant Walk,* about the English gentry lifestyle in Ceylon.

No other place I've seen gives a more realistic notion of how the coast of Georgia might have appeared to its first settlers than walking down the sandy road on Cumberland Island. I visited the cemetery where General Henry Lee (Lighthorse Harry), R. E. Lee's father, was buried in 1818. He fell ill aboard a ship, disembarked here, and died on the plantation. His remains were moved to Lexington in 1913. I continued walking to the beach, and along it a mile or so, before cutting back through the live oaks to the boat dock. I was able to identify several birds: the brown pelican, ringbilled gull, least tern, Bonaparte's gull, black and turkey vultures, anhinga, snowy egret, American oystercatchers, and sanderlings.

Although I'd kept up a pace on this trip, I wasn't tired in the stressful way I had been on the USA perimeter tour. Perhaps I was in better condition, and I had private time between social encounters, an impossibility when traveling with another person.

On the beach, I met the Millersville students again. They had seen Fort Clinch from the end of the island across St. Marys River and found

sand dollars on the beach. I sat down to watch the seagulls and got my pants wet, but they were dry by the time I got back to the boat.

I talked again with the volunteer guide, Cindy Bonnett. In response to my questions, she revealed that her husband had left her with three kids to raise. "You'll do well. The first few months are the worst and you've gotten through that," I said.

"Thanks," she said. "I think you're right."

When we docked at St. Marys, I unlocked my bicycle from the office fence, hopped aboard, and began spinning the pedals like mad to get home to the state park before dark! I arrived while the way was still visible. Thus, my second week on the road ended with great satisfaction. Tomorrow, I would pedal west for the first time.

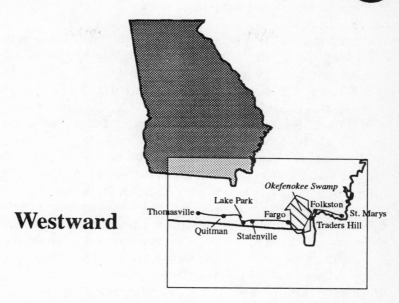

Westward

Crooked River State Park, Thursday, March 21

As I was taking down my tent, I couldn't help noticing Tonja and James Stahl, camped next to me. All through breakfast, she kept jumping up to see a pair of cardinals. Later, I met Tonja in the restroom and learned they are from Gatlinburg, Tennessee. Her response to life is vivacious. She expressed the wish that her mother would get out and do something like what I was doing.

"She's younger than you, too; you're not like a retired person."

Outside again, Tonja called my attention to a mourning dove with refreshing enthusiasm. Then she insisted James had to meet me. He laughed gently as he said that his woodwork "is a wonderful way not to make a living."

Pedaling out of camp, I noticed some vultures. The park ranger on Cumberland Island had noted that they never flap their wings if they don't have to, because the putrid food they eat contains few nutrients. Vultures won't eat anything alive, even if hungry. They soar to conserve energy.

It felt good to be on the road again, although I was fighting headwinds. Passing the McIntosh Sugar Mill Tabby Ruins, the largest and best-preserved tabby structure on the coast, I smiled; I'd seen enough tabby. Yes, I was ready to leave the coast for a time, and head west. While I pushed into the west wind, Tonja and James passed me in their truck. She yelled and waved like mad. It made me feel good, and I forgot about the headwind.

I pedaled on, recalling my visit to Gatlinburg, over 50 years ago, with my parents. It was my first trip to the Smoky Mountains, and to Clingman's Dome. The Gatlinburg I remembered was a one-road town with motels, restaurants, shops, and houses on both sides. Each end of town was forest. People in town kept pet bears on chains or in cages, some of them not much bigger than I was. Out on the road, if you stopped your car, the bears would approach. I remember giving a bear a Coke and watching it drink. Other bears came to beg for sweets. Wild bears rarely harmed anyone, certainly not without being provoked. While we were there, someone began to taunt a wild bear we were watching. My parents told me to get into the car. We departed, and I heard a lesson on the wrongs of teasing animals or people. My dad asked how I would like it if, after he poured my cereal in the morning, he handed me the milk, then took it away repeatedly. I understood; the lesson never needed repetition. Although cautious and respectful, I've never been afraid of black bears. I approach the ocean the same way. I think it is more important to teach caution than fear.

Before reaching the I-95 junction at Kingsland, I'd been thinking about pancakes at McDonald's, but found Kountry Family Restaurant across the street and turned in for their breakfast special of two eggs, grits, crisp bacon, toast, and decaffeinated coffee, washed down with three glasses of water.

While eating, I read about Georgia lake surface levels in the morning paper. Levels change a bit with rainfall and power production. Just 25 miles northwest of my starting point in Rabun County was Chatuge Lake. At 1,927 feet, it is the highest Georgia lake. Lake Burton, located near my Possum Trot house, is 1,865 feet. Lake Hartwell, close to where I spent my first night, is 660 feet. Lake Seminole, in southwest

Georgia, was the lowest lake surface listed in the paper at 77 feet. West Point Lake, at my halfway point north along the western state line, is 635 feet. The fall line, separating the Piedmont from the coastal plain, runs across Georgia from Augusta to Columbus. The difference between the West Point Lake water level, above Columbus, and of Lake George (190 feet), below Columbus, confirmed that I would cross the fall line during that sixty-mile stretch. The 440 foot dropoff had been apparent near Augusta. I could expect to climb it near Columbus as I returned north.

After breakfast, I waddled out to my bicycle and headed toward Folkston. While still in Kingsland, I passed the Theater Apartments, the most imaginative use for a small-town movie house I've seen. Usually, they are just closed and empty. I have seen announcements on old marquees for a dentist's office or community center. I remember wondering if the dentist had always wanted his name in lights. A sailor, just entering the apartments, told me they were new, each with its numbered parking space. He had just moved in, and thought the small efficiency units were reasonably priced and just fine for him. I guessed that having the submarine base nearby created a demand for all sorts of housing, making small apartments worth building.

At last I was really warm enough in shorts and a T-shirt! There were wild Cherokee roses in bloom and quite an assortment of butterflies, kept busy by the white lilies and wild yellow flowers that looked like black-eyed Susans with a yellow center. These roadside flowers were set off by a rich green background of planted pine trees. Every two rows of closely planted trees was separated by a tractor-wide space, mowed to keep down the palmetto and underbrush.

As I continued inland, the terrain changed from flat to slightly undulating. The ups were almost imperceptibly longer than the downs. I was headed from the almost-sea-level coast toward the Okefenokee Swamp, parallel to the convoluted St. Marys River. It made sense that I was going uphill. If the Swamp wasn't the highest area in southeast Georgia, it couldn't be the source of water for the Suwannee and St. Marys Rivers.

Carefully reading maps, and the data they provide, supplies more information than just road numbers and distances. For example, a person can make judgments about traffic density from the sizes of neighboring towns and the types and number of roads connecting them. What isn't apparent from the map alone is that in an area like Elbert County traffic consists of trucks hauling granite. Sand pits or fill dirt sources mean dump trucks, and one can expect logging trucks almost anywhere in south Georgia. If a person knows where sawmills, chip mills, and paper mills are, expectations can be even more precise.

At the Swamp visitor's center, I noticed that the Okefenokee swampwater ranges from 102 to 123 feet above sea level. Ninety percent of its runoff water goes to the Suwannee River; only ten percent feeds the St. Marys River. Even today, Okefenokee swampwater, which covers about 15 feet of decaying vegetation and peat that bubbles with gases, is pure enough to drink.

Two miles east of Folkston, on GA 40, I read an historical marker about Camp Pinckney, a short distance southwest. For many years, it was an important boat landing on the St. Marys River. Passengers and mail, traveling the Kings Road north from St. Augustine, crossed the river there by ferry. It was also an important landing for transferring freight being shipped by boat. Camp Pinckney is said to have been named for Captain Thomas Pinckney of South Carolina, who camped there with his troops on an expedition against the Lower Creek Indians. One of the first turpentine camps in this section was also located at Camp Pinckney.

After the marker, houses were more frequent. I saw a blinking light ahead, then passed a reduced speed sign. After traveling in a state for a time, the shape of signs gives you a feel for what is coming before the signs themselves are legible. A sign that reads, "Hardee's 1 mile" can tell you how far a major junction or city center will be, since fast food restaurants are usually located at congested strips or major junctions. The largest junction of highways near me was Folkston, named for the early settler and physician, Dr. William A. Folks.

I took an informal tour of Folkston, where neither bicycles nor horses are allowed on the sidewalk. Pedaling down Main Street, I noticed a "Hair Today" shop. I stopped to read the courthouse marker, which noted the creation of Charlton County in 1854, named for Judge Robert M. Charlton of Savannah. After the railroad began operation there, the county seat was moved to Folkston from Fort Alert.

Activity from old Center Village, two miles north, also moved to Folkston with the railroad. It had been a stagecoach stop on the Kings Road, and a trade center for surrounding county inhabitants who produced staple cotton, beeswax, honey, venison, hides, and furs, in exchange for flour, sugar, coffee, shot, powder, and other commodities they needed.

The Okefenokee Restaurant looked like the best lunch choice. When I went into the restroom, I was shocked at how silly I looked wearing my T-shirt wrong side out. It was neon green, and the back had faded in the sun. This morning, I'd put it on inside out to fade it more evenly, and provide a brighter beacon as I pedaled where vehicle drivers weren't expecting a bicyclist. Turning the shirt right side out probably didn't improve my appearance much, but I felt better about sitting in the restaurant that way. The buffet offered not only two meats but a multitude of vegetables. I ate so many hot vegetables I couldn't think about salad and soup.

I wouldn't have eaten so much if I hadn't known how close I was to the Trader's Hill County Campground. When I arrived there in mid-afternoon, I found two motor homes and a trailer, but no people. I set up my tent and put my things inside. A marker told me the place had been a refuge for settlers during the Indian Wars, and Fort Alert had been built on this site. Now called Traders Hill, in 1901 it had been the head of navigation on the St. Marys River, and one of the most important centers in the southeast.

I took off to the old town site, to see the Methodist Church and the cemetery, where many pioneers of the region were buried. Then I rolled down to the bottom of the hill to see the river landing. When I returned to camp, there were people about. One person told me this landing had been used in the recent drug trade, which was decreasing.

I had caught a cold, so I took a couple of aspirin, ate crackers and a food bar called Meal-to-Go for supper, and drank a water bottle full of instant cider. I hadn't been drinking enough water recently; I drank several bottles of it throughout the afternoon. The air was soft and balmy as I read *Lighthouse* by Eugenia Price, an historical novel about St. Simons Island and this area during the earliest days of settlement.

The man in charge of the camp said I might not like the sulphur water. I laughed, and told him it reminded me of the first time I ever stayed in a hotel. Before I started school, my aunt and uncle took me to St. Augustine. I was impressed by two things, the fort and the sulphur water. I learned to drink it and brush my teeth with it as usual; it has never bothered me since.

Trader's Hill Campground, Friday, March 22

A day off the pedals meant using the bicycle just for errands, not loaded for travel from city to city. The day began with fruit in my tent and an attempt to catch up on note-taking. The Haddens, my neighbors in the trailer, invited me for coffee. They live in Brunswick and come here for about two weeks a year. They stay through Easter, and relatives come to visit. Mr. Hadden is retired from the U.S. Navy and slightly crippled. His daughter cares for him.

I left at mid-morning. It took me an hour to reach the Okefenokee National Wildlife Refuge Suwannee Canal. While paying the entry fee, I met Steven Weyl from Atlanta. He was traveling on a motorcycle and planned to rent a canoe for his first visit to the swamp.

I took the tourist boat along the canal and into some of the prairie areas. Our guide said we were 17 miles, in a straight flight line, from the Stephen Foster State Park at the center of the swamp. The canal, he said, had been dug ten miles inland in an attempt to drain swampwater and convert the land to farms. It didn't work. There had been a lot of rain recently, making the swampwater anywhere from one to three feet deep. The canal itself normally ran five to seven feet in depth. Swampwater reflects well because of its tannic acid content (which also explains its tea color). I got a good photo of a golden club lily and an alligator.

The tie-tie bushes that line the canal belong to the azalea family. They bloom in May, making the tour a beautiful voyage. Bees make excellent honey from the blossoms. The cypress trees in the swamp are fairly young and small, though they can grow to heights of 150 feet, with eleven-foot-thick trunks. The large, old cypress trees were cut by loggers between 1900 and 1935. They grow so slowly — less than half an inch a year — that we will not see full-grown trees in our lifetime. I like the lacy quality of the leaves and the tiny delicate cones.

It was interesting to come to the Okefenokee again. On my only other visit, I crossed it by canoe with five experienced canoeists from Maryland. This time, I really wanted to go to the visitor's centers and exhibits at Waycross, but was too lazy to make the round trip of over a hundred miles. I added them to my "come back" list, then justified the decision, telling myself the road was heavily traveled by large trucks.

After the relaxing and amusing motorboat tour, I watched all the films at the visitor's center and bought a book, *History of Okefenokee*. I credited my laziness to what I believed was a head cold, which I treated with lots of fluids. I consumed a half-gallon of grapefruit juice, and more than that of water during the day. I'd been taking KM, a mineral supplement of 14 natural herbs and lots of potassium, but I was running low. The support system set up to send me a new supply didn't work out, so I'd cut my normal intake in half.

Restored by being inside, out of the sun, entertained, and educated about the area, I filled my water bottles at the drinking fountain and climbed on my bike to take the nine-mile tourist drive that led to boardwalk tours and observation platforms. I wandered about a restored homestead farm, set among the pine trees. En route, I saw underbrush being burned to promote growth. It smelled good and was still smoking in places, even burning here and there. Spring is the best time for scheduled burns.

I saw a few alligators, several wild flowers, and a lot more pine trees, but the highlights of the day were marvelous views of pileated woodpeckers.

Herons were abundant here, as they had been in the roadside water channels all along my route. The great blue heron, for example, I saw at least once a day, either standing still so I wouldn't notice, or flying off as a result of my passage.

On the boardwalk and in the observation tower, the wildlife was rather still in mid-afternoon, but the views were fine, and the people were interesting. I met a fellow from Rockville, Maryland, on vacation from his job with the Giant grocery store chain, and on spring break from college. We thought we recognized each other from Cumberland Island. A couple from New Mexico, who had been to a conference in Washington, D.C., were touring a bit before returning home.

Another couple I met examining a personnel counter on the boardwalk were taking a six-month tour of America. His parents died several years ago, leaving him some money. The couple decided to pack up and wander and photograph America this year, using some of the money he inherited. By profession, he is a machinist; he carried some impressive photographic equipment.

I pedaled home to Trader's Hill and rested before cooking supper and my bicycle chain, which had squeaked all day. I had decided on couscous for supper, a pasta that takes the least fuel to cook and is lightweight. Lifting the pot off the stove, I looked up as a car stopped with two men and a boy inside. The driver rolled down the window and said, "We saw your bicycle and wonder where you are from? I'm a bicyclist too, but haven't been out much this year. I've got a lot of parts and tools if you need anything." When he stopped talking I gave a few short answers without much enthusiasm; I was tired and hungry. While they got out of the car, I put the pan with my chain on the stove, so as not to have to turn it off or waste fuel.

Amos McMillan introduced himself, his friend Pete Minor, and Peter's five-year-old son, Nathan. The men were pastors. Amos had heard of cooking a bicycle chain but had not seen it done. He asked questions while he watched. He said paraffin is apparently making a comeback. Pete suggested putting a little graphite in it, and stirring it well while it melted. I thought that might be a good idea, and told him I often put in STP oil treatment — not much, or the paraffin would be too soft. Pete had heard plain engine oil recommended as an additive.

Amos was surprised I hadn't ever broken more than one or two spokes. He had broken three spokes in 5,000 miles, probably, he said, "because I'm heavy." I laughed. "You could lose weight or rebuild the wheel with heavier-gauge spokes; from my experience, the second would be easier!" He invited me to attend his church, and wished me well on my journey. I'd enjoyed the visit but wished I hadn't been so hungry. As soon as they left, instead of cooking the other chain as intended, I opened a tin of chicken, dumped it in the now-cold couscous, and ate it.

The man who cared for the camp, J. L. Wheeler, later told me that he had walked over to see who those people were. I had seen him do it. When he realized it was Amos, he knew I was safe. When I saw him return to the office, I knew he thought the people were OK. J.L. was particularly careful to watch anyone who came near my tent. I appreciated that, because the campground was right on the road to the river at the bottom of the hill. Everyone else in the campground was worried about my safety, too, so I didn't need to think about it much. I'd assumed I was watched from nearby trailers, and sure enough the Haddens, during coffee that morning, had told me everything I did after I came out of the tent.

It was now dark, and I had settled down to read. Another visitor came. When I first returned to camp in the afternoon, I had spoken with a couple from Canada, Gusti Adams and her husband. The Adamses spoke fast "Yankee," with a slight Germanic or Yiddish lilt, and had difficulty understanding the language of the campground managers. They wanted to canoe on the river and arrange for someone to pick them up afterward and return them to their car. One of the camp men had a truck, and was glad to help out, but they were having difficulty communicating. I had no trouble understanding everybody, so I acted as interpreter. I had had early training in the difficulties caused by unusual accents when my family moved from Georgia to Ohio when I was eleven. In Ohio, no one at school could understand my accent. Teachers called on me, but couldn't understand what I said. Other students, giving the same reply, got credited with knowing the answer. Between classes, the other kids smiled at me and urged me to "say something." They obviously liked my southern accent, but couldn't understand the words. I did poorly in school and became self-conscious, quiet, observant, a mimic, and, later, a clown.

I thought J. L. and the other camp manager had clearly agreed to meet the Adamses tomorrow. They only wanted to know where and when to meet. The Adamses, who said they would pay for the service, were repeating and reaffirming everything. They didn't appear to understand the nonverbal cues, especially the southern nods and mumbles or silences, which were rather subtle signs of agreement. They apparently didn't understand that these were small-town men whose nod was a bond. The Adamses followed me to my tent and asked if the southern men were reliable. I told them not to worry, and assured them I'd eaten at the Okefenokee Restaurant, which had been recommended by the men.

Since they were coming back to camp after their trip, I asked them to bring a certain type of flashlight battery, if they happened into a store, but not to go searching. My after dark-visitor was Gusti Adams, with the batteries. I was delighted and reimbursed her. They had decided to stay in town for the night. The camp managers had gone for the night, and she wanted me to tell the man who would pick them up after their canoe trip that they would come to the camp about 9:30 A.M. to complete arrangements.

Trader's Hill County Campground, Saturday, March 23

At 3:00 a.m. I awoke, ate a banana, then went back to sleep. About 6:00 A.M., when I heard two sets of "who cooks for you" from the owl, I awoke for the day and ate the rest of my grapes. I had to get up and get going. It would be a long pedal around the swamp, especially if I went all the way to Valdosta or into the center of the swamp, to Stephen

Foster State Park. They were the only places I knew of to stay. While I was stowing my tent, the Haddens called over and invited me for coffee. We agreed I would finish packing first. When I knocked on their trailer door, I was ready to travel. Jackie and E. L. Haden were eating breakfast. Jackie fixed me a plate of two scrambled eggs, two pieces of toast, sausage, and coffee. They told me there was a motel in Fargo, and where stores were located along the desolate road. They had watched me pack and couldn't believe I got the whole tent into that small bag and hung all that stuff on the bicycle. I said goodbye, thanked them, and pushed the bike through the sand, stopping to talk to the camp manager who had agreed to meet the Adamses. I forgot to tell him they were coming at 9:30 A.M. to see him.

A little way down the road, perhaps a mile or so, I passed J.L.'s house. He came out to wish me well and, in the course of conversation, told me about coming over when the pastors came to my tent last night and going away when he realized who they were. Bingo! I remembered the message about the Adamses. I hopped on my bike and headed back to tell the man with the truck not to leave before the canoeists came. Long before I reached the crossroad, I saw his vehicle turn down the road to town. I returned to J.L.'s house to ask if he could phone the other man. He said he would take care of it, for he knew the fellow would like to help. Finally, I was on my way to the highway.

At Trader's Hill, the air under Hangman's Oak, and other hundreds-of-years-old live oaks, had been very still, but a few miles of pedaling put me on GA 23 south into a steady headwind. Rolling toward St. George, I averaged only about ten miles an hour, not my intended speed. I reached the post office about 10:30. First, there was a line. Then, the postman and a woman wanted to know who I was and where I was going. About that time, two young men on good bikes, in brilliant jerseys and riding shorts, stopped to talk. I still had not taken my package out of the pannier.

The two young men, Greg Pratt and Rob Jessup, were in the Navy. One was a pilot, the other a navigator. Both men had missed going to Saudi Arabia because they hadn't finished training in time. They told me that servicemen on active duty in America at the time would receive a ribbon and medal. They wanted to do some cross-country touring, and quizzed me about sources of information. I suggested the League of American Wheelmen *Almanac* that lists bicycle clubs and rides all over the country. If their plane was big enough to carry their bicycles when they went on training flights, they could pedal on the ground and easily use the almanac to find local bicyclists who would know routes. Today, they were doing a circle tour of about 50 miles on GA highways 185, 94, and 121, and had driven to their starting place from Jacksonville. They didn't mention that they were traveling with the wind.

After finally mailing a package of heavy clothes to Sue Smith in Columbus, I went over to the grocery to get a few bananas for the rest of the day. In the IGA grocery window was a small sign — "Welcome Bicycle Tourists - BikeCentennial." Obviously St. George was on a tour route of BikeCentennial, another national organization that sells maps and provides an annual "Bicyclists' Yellow Pages" of tour organizers, clubs, and rides.

Both the League of American Wheelmen and BikeCentennial produce magazines for about 25,000 members, a third of them common to both. It seems a shame to me that many bicycle organizations have splintered so that groups compete for membership. I often think how fine a magazine bicyclists would enjoy if the funds spent on these two were combined.

A loaded touring bicyclist pedaled by just as I was about to leave the junction at St. George. He waved, but showed no inclination to halt. Half as loaded as I and pushed by a tailwind, he was moving well, proceeding north.

I'd been at the junction an hour. My leg muscles, unaccustomed to long halts, seemed to think they had done their work for the day and were reluctant to proceed, especially when I'd gone about fifty feet and realized that the headwind coming south had been a mere nothing compared to the one I faced pedaling west. It was going to be a long, hard afternoon. I looked down GA 94, knowing it stretched forty miles to Fargo, and I knew I'd get no further than that today. Winds tend to strengthen in the afternoon.

There were signs on the pine forest trees that Gilman Paper Company owned the land, and that it was used by the Georgia Bend Hunting Club. But I was alone among the pine trees, glad I was wearing a long-sleeved cotton shirt. It had gotten quite hot and sunny, and my left side, leg, face, and hand turned red, in spite of sun-block cream. I was grateful for Solarcaine.

White and purple thistles along the road attracted small, round-winged, yellow butterflies, as well as large, black, pointed-winged ones with yellow spots that looked to be of the monarch family. There were large, buzzing bumblebees and one pileated woodpecker. One large bird might have been a golden eagle, or maybe one of the hawk family.

After a time, I began practicing ankle and pedaling circles to improve my rhythm by making the legs, ankles, and feet flex and push me ahead. I've long had the bad habit of using a stiff-ankle rotation.

Though I had seen many signs of recent rain, I was surprised to see the river so far out of its banks as I came across the Suwannee River into Fargo. It submerged some of the picnic tables and barbecue pits, and almost the whole park.

There was no decision to be made. I was exhausted, and happy to stay at the Gator Motel, which was clean and comfortable. Fargo isn't very large. A few steps away were a phone booth, which I used, and a restaurant, where I enjoyed supper of two fried catfish, baked potatoes, cole slaw, and gallons of cold water. A hot shower revived me, but I was quite content to recline in bed and read until I fell asleep.

I entertained no further thoughts of reentering the swamp for it was now clear that I would have headwinds most of the way westward across south Georgia, and would not make my expected distances or speeds. Wind seems to tire me more than struggling up hills; there is no exhilarating descent on the other side. The side trips to Albany and Plains I'd thought about were no longer of interest. I'd stick to the perimeter and be satisfied. Everything else was relegated by fatigue to the "next trip" list.

Gator Motel, Fargo, Sunday, March 24

With my side-trip plans wiped out, time wasn't so critical. It was Sunday and I spent the morning peacefully writing notes and reading until checkout time. The day before, I'd bought fruit and some snacks before the store across the street closed. Often in small towns, nothing is open on Sunday. Here, fishermen, hunters, and other outdoor people were about on weekends, so the groceries and gas stations were open, although they were far apart.

The post office flag across the street hung limply down its pole. The sky was cloudy, which suited me; I'd gotten quite enough sun yesterday. I pedaled out of town about 11:00 A.M. headed for Statenville, 30 miles ahead. I expected to pass nothing but creeks and pine trees on the way. Once I was on the road, there was a headwind, but not as strong as yesterday afternoon. The road was mostly flat, vegetation was like yesterday, and there seemed to be more curves in the road.

At one place, a deer walked up to the edge of the road ahead of me, stopped, looked both ways, saw me, and scampered across into the woods. I counted utility poles to the place where the deer crossed and measured the distance with my Avocet at .2 miles. At the next bridge, I stopped, leaned my bike on the rail, and cut an apple with the Swiss knife Frances Porcher had brought me from Geneva. She had even had my name imprinted on it. I was about nine miles from Statenville, and the wind was getting stronger. I chewed the apple and observed the water flowing below the bridge: no fish, turtles, or snakes.

I decided not to go to Valdosta, which would take me north an additional ten miles. Instead, I would continue due west to Lake Park, where there were stores and a good campground. I'd seen enough white ibis, snowy egrets, and butterflies, as well as herons and cattle egrets. I remembered how boring this road had been when I drove it by car, at five times my present speed, to meet the canoeists for our swamp tour. The road, planted in pine trees, goes for miles like a causeway through the lowland. There were recently burnt underbrush, cut underbrush, palmetto, and lilies in bloom, as well as wildflowers along the road. Standing water filled every low place.

As I came to Statenville, wisteria was in bloom. Its scent, carried on the breeze, smelled wonderful, filling the whole countryside even when I couldn't see it. Eating a few snacks — a V8 juice, a Klondike ice cream bar, and a package of strawberry wafers — I reconfirmed the decision to head for Lake Park.

Leaving town, I crossed the Alapaha River, which a postmistress had recommended for canoeing. Pastures with fine horses reminded me of last fall's Florida Bicycle Safari near Ocala. I came into Lake Park with a wonderful breeze. It was cool, balmy, and pleasantly mid-80s. I passed the "Cut N Run" beauty and barber shop, and found the Eagles Roost Campground.

The man at the desk graciously gave me a few dollars discount off the mobile home price. A woman who looked like an unusually pleasant person registered ahead of me. Pedaling around to pick a site, I noticed her and her husband, also pleasant looking, unhooking their car. I took the site next door, we nodded, and I began to put up my tent. The site had a tree, which I like, because I can pitch my tent so the leaves keep off dew. There did not appear to be any bright streetlights nearby to keep me awake, either.

The woman came over and asked me to have supper with them. I accepted quickly, after two days of nothing but pine trees for company. Norma Smith introduced herself and her husband, Robin. She said she was driving to the store later, and asked if I needed anything. I went with her and bought yogurt, crackers, bananas, and grapes for breakfast. Norma was interested in checking out the outlets so we walked in and out of a number of them. The Tog Shop Outlet caught my eye and since I'd read their catalog for years but never managed to get to the shop, I was glad to wander in there. We were pleasantly surprised by the quality of the merchandise.

The Smiths weren't going far tomorrow, only to Clemson to see friends from South Carolina. It seemed a world away for me, about two weeks by bicycle. As a rule of thumb, I could travel in a day what a car would do in an hour.

Back at camp, while I was arranging things on the bike and in the tent, a couple from Michigan stopped to ask about bicycling. They were in their 70s, and both had bikes with them. They worried about saddle soreness. I explained about the riding pants with padding inside, and the importance of adjusting the seat and handlebars for comfort on even a short ride. Since they were from Michigan, I recommended the Shoreline ride the next summer. They wanted me to look at their bicycles. It seemed to me they needed to pedal, not necessarily far, but daily, to build up their ability. I also suggested they join a club at home to find other people who rode at their level and would know routes they would enjoy.

During supper, Robin and Norma Smith told me about their five children. The last two, twin boys, now work in the electric business Robin runs. We ate grilled hamburgers with tomato and mustard, ten-bean salad, fresh corn, and fresh strawberries. Their warm company made a lovely time for me. We talked about routes and campgrounds and things we liked to do and see on the road. They were on a two-week vacation in their motor home, and were towing a small car. Norma was not satisfied with the strawberries, which she thought not ripe enough, and was glad to give me what we had not eaten. I put them in my yogurt and ate them just before going to sleep.

On an after supper-walk around the camp, I met William and Rosalie Butson from Warren, Michigan. I'd once escorted a group to look at tanks being manufactured and tested there. We reminisced about the cinnamon buns sold in the upper peninsula of Michigan. The Smiths and Butsons gave me a fun and joyful evening.

Finally, the long, happy day ended. I stretched out in the tent and made a list of things to do before departure in the morning. I needed to pump the tires, record yesterday's miles (43), and call Earl Johnson, who lived in Roswell, north of Atlanta. He wanted to ride a few days with me but we were having trouble getting our schedules to fit, especially as I didn't have a fixed agenda. His wife Diane had come to my talk and slide show at REI (Recreation Equipment, Inc.) in Atlanta, but I hadn't yet met Earl. On the phone, the Johnsons agreed we would meet north of Columbus. Diane would drive Earl to our starting point and pick him up later, carrying all my stuff in the meantime. It sounded like a splendid plan. I was to call them again in about ten days to pin down the details.

Lake Park, Eagles Roost Campground, Monday, March 25

I met William and Rosalie Butson on my way to the bathhouse, and they gave me a newspaper article about a man with a lung illness who was riding the perimeter of the USA.

Shortly before 8:00 A.M. I pedaled away from camp, taking GA 376, and was soon in the country. I saw a red bird that might have been a summer tanager, then another, more brilliant bird, whose distinct black wings and tail indicated a scarlet tanager. My nose and my attention were attracted by a large mill that smelled like wet, warm paste. In Clyattville, at the store at the junction of GA 376 and GA 31, Mary Ann Smith confirmed that my nose had detected a paper mill. I bought some Smartfood popcorn, which I hadn't seen for some time. Mary Ann also gave me splendid directions to Quitman, so I continued on GA 31 west to Nankin Road, then north on GA 33. Red clover was in bloom along the way, the farms and homes were interesting, and the birds talked among themselves.

Even though I seemed to be climbing gradually, the day before I had been able to pedal between 7 and 12 miles per hour. Today's pace was an encouraging 12 to 16 miles per hour. Every now and then on a downhill, for an exhilarating moment, I got up to 20 miles per hour! I saw a lot of birds flying away from my bicycle — woodpeckers, blue jays, whippoorwills. Pasture and woods alternated. I saw a small falcon; maybe someday I'll learn to recognize them in flight. There was a two-story log cabin, still used as a home. Suddenly, a sort of "burr conflutter" occurred — I'd flushed a covey of quail — lovely! An old wagon sat on the porch of a house shaded by pecan trees. Though soft and gentle, I had a tailwind!

The best thing about turning north on GA 33 was that it put my left leg in shadow and gave sun to the other calf. My left leg would have been mooing along with the cows I was passing, if it hadn't gotten some shade. Pedaling in a long-sleeved sweatshirt was just right, as it kept sun off my arms, but when I stopped it was too hot.

I went past a couple of peach orchards, one with the leaves just coming and the other still showing a few blossoms. At the turn north, about two miles from the Florida line, I began climbing.

I passed an eight-section irrigating machine, sitting idle in a field like a giant grasshopper. Last year I'd seen them in use. They move so slowly while spraying water that I didn't realize the wheels were turning until I stopped to take a photo and the machine kept going — at about half the speed of a second hand on a watch.

I saw a hawk — I think it was a red-tail — quite close. I stopped the bike on the grass, pulled out my binoculars, and began to watch it circle. I felt something chewing on my leg, and looked down to see that I had stepped on top of an ant hill! Birdwatching succumbed to stomping the ants off my foot and leg and pedaling on, with a few more shakes and scratches. The sting only lasted about ten minutes.

During this trip, I passed a lot of dumpsters, often with people looking through them for food. We throw away so much usable food in this country. In Atlanta, and perhaps other cities, there are organized pickups of outdated food which is no longer legal for grocery stores to sell. The food is given to the homeless, through various charitable organizations. There are, however, large, covered and locked dumpsters

— compactors — that some grocery chains use. The food discarded in them is immediately crushed, of no use to anyone. I have a friend who considers it recreation to visit a grocery dumpster and cull the useable food by date or quality. She gets vegetables, yogurt, milk, juices, large quanities of bread, and when it is cold enough, ice cream. She distributes some to her family, but most goes to the poor of her church. They carefully throw away anything spoiled; no one has ever gotten sick. I tried to estimate, and credit her with feeding fifty to a hundred people a week!

I asked at a boarding house once if they had to throw away all the uneaten food set on a table in serving dishes. Legally they must, I was told, but the people who work in the kitchen sometimes tote it home, which helps a bit. I'm not against laws enacted for health reasons, but I do wonder about the food lost to the homeless and hungry. At any rate, I'm an advocate of following the spirit rather than the letter of the law in certain circumstances.

I knew I was nearing Quitman when I heard the train whistle travel from east to west ahead of me. On the map the train tracks went through town. I rounded a curve and entered Quitman, a town built around one of the courthouse squares which are so common in Georgia. I pedaled around, looked at some of the lovely old homes, then stopped in the Chamber of Commerce, where Shirley Bell told me about the town and suggested several restaurants.

I decided on the Georgian Motel Restaurant across the street, and walked in five minutes before it was officially open for lunch. The lunch buffet was a splendid hot meal, worthy of the old southern habit of eating dinner in the middle of the day. I was hungry again for green beans, potatoes, smothered steak, cornbread, and apple cobbler. I would have preferred a few more vegetables, but ate a salad instead.

Riding through town after lunch, I admired the dogwood, azaleas, and wisteria, as well as the homes. The people of Quitman had "adopted" the highways all the way to the county line, in all directions. Their civic pride was evident in yards and homes as I pedaled part of the route of a house tour. I decided I'd better keep pedaling. I'd eaten so much I might fall asleep on a park bench if I halted.

On the highway again, headed for Thomasville, I watched two crows chasing a hawk, but had to pay attention to the road, for there was more traffic. As I went by Dixie, a bus full of people passed me, and

I looked to see where they were going: America. Nervous truck drivers gave me a bit of air horn as they passed, and I had to get off onto the grass shoulder a couple of times, where there were no paved shoulders.

Pecan trees hadn't even thought about leaves yet, but a few chinaberry trees were green. Spring was exploding with the aroma of wisteria. I spent the early afternoon watching mockingbirds, vultures, and crows.

By 2:15 P.M., I was registered in a campground on the outskirts of Thomasville. There were no trees, so I put up my tent knowing it would get wet with dew in the night, and stowed my gear. Then I hopped on my bike and headed for the Thomasville Museum, two miles west. The whole town smelled like wisteria. Azaleas and dogwood were at their peak, and I almost fell off my bike looking at one of the beautiful yards instead of where I was going. Then I nearly ran into the curb watching a pair of red-headed woodpeckers in a magnolia tree.

Finally, I came to the Historical Society Museum, where Margaret Ellis took me to join a tour being conducted by Curator C. Tom Hill, raconteur and historian. He was explaining that costs, compared to what a day's wages would buy in necessary goods today, are about the same as in colonial times. The Thomasville area, he continued, was the highest point (330 feet) in southern Georgia. It had become a resort for the rich about 15 years before Jekyll Island attracted their attention.

One reason for the area's exceptional prosperity was the quality of the soil, which used to produced more and finer cotton per acre than anywhere else in Georgia. There was good access to transportation: roads to Tallahassee were suitable for wagons, and the railroad from there to the sea was economically practical.

In this century, the enormous plantations grow nothing. They are used for hunting and relaxed entertaining. The guest hunter always goes away having shot better than ever before in his life. The guides carefully observe his ability. Then a professional marksman stands near the guest and if, after a time, he fails to get a hit, the marksman shoots so well synchronized with the hunter that he believes he has succeeded.

Outside, on the museum grounds, we saw two examples of 18th-century homes. One was the 100-year-old city home of an average, educated person. The other, a log house, was reassembled on the museum grounds to show how a farmer without slaves lived. Tom explained that log cabins had an earth floor; this was a log house because it was built a foot or so off the ground with a wood floor.

He noted that the space between the logs was not stuffed with dirt, clay, or anything to make the house airtight. Here in south Georgia, the winters are not that cold, and the summers are too hot to live in a home that has no air passing through it. The wood that was cut off the logs when they were being squared was nailed on the inside between the logs. Still, there were many places where we could see daylight through the living room walls. This allowed the house to breathe. It had a high ceiling. You might think it would be difficult to heat or that loft space would be needed for the children to sleep. Not so. Any child sleeping up there in summer would roast.

The log house had two rooms: a living room and a slightly smaller bedroom. Cooking was done over the fireplace. Chairs were hung on the wall at night, providing plenty of floor space for pallets for the children. The parents and babies slept in the bedroom. However, the bed would come apart and fold out of the way to allow space for children to play on rainy days. In summer, children often slept on the front porch. Boards laid across sawhorses, inside the living room in winter and outside in summer, were the dining table. Between meals, table-boards and sawhorses were stored under the house. This custom is the origin of the term "room and board." Later, the term expanded to "boarding house," referring to a place where you ate and slept.

Tom Hill assured us that if we returned to visit this house in August, the temperature would be 20 or more degrees cooler inside. He had measured it several times. Someone asked about the insects. Yes, he admitted, they come in, but the large animals stay out. There was glass in the windows of the living room, with shutters outside, but the bedroom had only wooden shutters.

Tom pointed out that in the antebellum South there was almost no middle class. That is one reason a middle-class house of this type is so rare. Tom told us that only the ultra-rich had slaves, because buying and keeping them was expensive. People who could afford slaves owned plantation tracts of land (thousands of acres or square miles). Furnishings for their homes were imported from England and France. The house we were in belonged to a settler who had 500 acres he and his family worked. He had a dozen children, typical of farm families. One-third of the children would die before adulthood if the farm did well, perhaps half would die if it did not.

Very few families were wealthy enough to own more than 50 slaves. For dangerous work, hired labor was used, slaves being too valuable. In antebellum times, rice and cotton were so labor intensive, landowners could not have grown them successfully without slaves. I couldn't help wondering what Georgia's history might have been if slaves had never come there. Probably there would have been nothing for Sherman's troops to burn.

Thomasville was founded in 1832. Its heyday, 1870 to 1906, was known as the hotel era. People came for their health because Thomasville was high enough to escape the mosquitoes that carried yellow fever and malaria. During the hotel era, the *very* wealthy found they could own a plantation for the cost of supporting a large entourage in a hotel for a couple of months. Fifteen years later, after the Panama Canal experience showed that draining swamps could improve health, some of these same families established a resort at Jekyll Island. About the same time, the railroad in Florida reached Miami, and competition with southern Florida abruptly ended Thomasville's time in the resort spotlight.

The generosity of rich families who continued coming to Thomasville contributed to the town's prosperity. For example, the Archibalds gave the town a complete hospital — land, building, equipment, staff, and operating funds.

Full-time residents of Thomasville have learned how to cater to the whims of the rich when they visit their plantations. Building on these skills, the town has developed a successful tourist industry, including the annual Rose Festival. Thomasville has a strong English influence, complete with hunting dogs and horses brought over from England and Scotland. The area offers a safe refuge — if you know the right people. For example, Jacqueline Kennedy spent several weeks there after President Kennedy was shot.

I bought some fruit at the State Farmers Market (certainly more fun than a grocery), returned to my tent just before dark, and ate supper from supplies on hand.

Thomasville, RV Park, Tuesday, March 26

By 9:30 A.M., I was on the bike, headed for Pebble Hill Plantation — without my helmet. My just-washed hair was dry and wavy, and I just couldn't face another day of mashed and sweaty helmet-hair. The morning was fine, the air champagne-fresh, clean, crisp, and full of wisteria sweetness.

I took Pinetree Boulevard around the south side of town and looked at everyone's yard as I went by. People were most particular about their gardens, which were a joy to observe.

Many towns claim to be the friendliest, the most interesting, the most historic, or the best-kept secret in Georgia. Thomasville may qualify for all of the above. The clear air indicates how, in days of no air conditioning, this could have been a resort. I went by Forbes Drive, which leads to Thomas College, founded in 1950, then passed the Millpond Plantation's beautiful gate of blooming wisteria.

A garbage truck passed me. A sign on the side said: "Litter—a thorn among our roses." The biggest event of the year is the Rose Festival at the end of April. The Rose Test Garden is one of 25 official test gardens in the United States. I was a few weeks too early; it had not yet opened.

Throughout south Georgia I'd enjoyed the wild Cherokee Rose, a fragrant, white flower on a prickly, climbing shrub which is Georgia's state flower. Originally from China, it was introduced to England in 1756, and brought to Georgia a few years later. Renamed here for the Cherokee Indians, the largest tribe in the southeastern United States, the rose grows wild in every county in Georgia. This prompted a federation of women's clubs to propose its adoption as Georgia's official flower. Approval by the state legislature came on August 18, 1916.

There are still over 70 plantations in the Thomasville area, and, it seemed, examples of every type of architectural style in Georgia. At Pebble Hill Plantation, I pedaled into an era reminiscent of the palaces of Europe. Elizabeth Ireland Poe, "Miss Pansy," was the one of the Hanna family of Cleveland, and an avid sportswoman, hostess, collector, and patron of the arts. She willed her home, except her bedroom, to be open to the public upon her death. Any outdoor person, especially someone who likes dogs or horses, should visit Miss Pansy's place.

She collected stirrup cups, lamps, prints, sculpture, and place-card holders in silver, glass, and pewter. Horse heads and hunting dogs that are used in any type of art will be found somewhere in the Pebble Hill house. The Audubon prints alone are worth a visit. It feels and looks like she still lives there.

Then there were the gardens and the architecture of the house and stables. Everywhere I looked there was something of artistic merit. One of her prize cows actually had a gravestone inscribed "Mother Superior." By the time I'd seen as much as I could absorb, I was indeed grateful to Miss Pansy for the opportunity.

Mistletoe

One could imagine such a life would be easy, but I think it requires discipline and commitment to be fulfilling. Life is not easy for anyone. If the purpose of life is learning, it is not supposed to be easy. We need pressure to motivate us. Willingness to learn is the most difficult thing in the world to maintain. It is particularly hard to learn without admitting there might be something you don't know.

It was mid-afternoon when I reached town, hungry for lunch. Doris' Home Cooking hadn't closed up yet and still had some vegetables. Rested and restored, I found the Big Oak which has grown in Thomasville since about 1685 on two-thirds of an acre of land near the post office.

I wasn't too late, but the Lapham-Patterson House had not attracted any other tourists that afternoon, and it was closed. I was disappointed, but returned instead to Thomas County Historical Society and Museum for a slide show and talk about the Thomasville Army Air Base during World War II.

I pedaled back to camp, cleaned up a bit, and went to Mom and Dad's Italian Restaurant for eggplant parmesan with spaghetti. Either dish would have been enough. Naturally, I ate every bite of both and returned again to camp, riding on the sidewalk in the dark.

The camp manager invited me to sit in the game room and watch TV for the evening. I set up my computer and typed notes until 10:00 P.M. without finishing them. Then I cooked my chain and put it back on the bike. It had been clicking, clacking, and squeaking. When I crawled into my sleeping bag, sleep came at once.

Thomasville, RV Campground, Wednesday, March 27

US 84 West was a fine road, four lanes with a paved shoulder much of the way. It was graded for trucks, so I moved happily to Cairo (pronounced like the syrup, not like the city in Egypt). During a mid-morning breakfast of eggs, bacon, grits, and biscuits, with decaffeinated coffee, a retired truck driver and his wife in a nearby booth asked about my means of travel. They were long-time residents of Cairo, and he was a man who thought in highway numbers, having traveled the local roads throughout his career. He gave me excellent directions for biking through town instead of bypassing it. When I asked what I should know about Cairo he told me Roddenbery's Pickle Factory made the best peanut butter anywhere!

A businessman who sat nearby volunteered that he was a peanut farmer from the Suffolk, Virginia area. There had been rain, and they had a wonderful crop this year. When he shifted to his son's high school activities I began to edge toward the door, for I had a long way to pedal.

I mailed a package to my friend, Sue Smith, in Columbus. She would drive to my mountain house in Possum Trot to meet me after the tour. I couldn't mail things to myself at General Delivery because no one would pick them up in time.

Between Cairo and Bainbridge, the day and road were so fine I sped through a crosswind that only seldom shifted to a headwind or tailwind. As in sailing a boat, the forward motion of the bicycle creates an apparent wind. Its direction appears to vary slightly with speed. I was glad this was my last day of proceeding west.

I'd left the fine quail-hunting areas near Cairo behind by the time I stopped to photograph a farm I named Mistletoe Hill. I'd been looking for a tree with a lot of mistletoe and no leaves, standing in good light, so the picture would illustrate how easy it is to identify. While giving slide shows, I discovered that many people have never seen mistletoe growing. Some don't know it grows in trees, or they don't recognize it. It is so common in Georgia that I remember it from childhood and have no trouble spotting it among the tree branches.

As I continued past Whigham and Climax, parallel to the railroad, the pecan tree farms gave way to open field farms and pasture. Then I roared down an escarpment at 32 miles per hour and came to a halt at a Food Lion on the outskirts of Bainbridge. It was early afternoon. I bought three yogurts, a head of lettuce, three small cans of tuna fish, and supplies for camping. It was 84 degrees outside. I ate all three yogurts, so they wouldn't spoil. Well, it was lunch! Riding quietly, I admired the restored Victorian homes of Bainbridge.

The night before the camp manager had told me a story about Bainbridge. People had come to his camp after midnight, in a frightened state. In a motor home, they had halted at the public campground under the Flint River Bridge in Bainbridge. After dark a large group of youths circled their camp. Although perhaps an isolated incident, he recommended I not stay there alone. Recalling his advice as I pedaled over the Flint River, I looked over the bridge and saw an inviting camping area. It was empty, not unusual for midday and mid-week. I hadn't thought to ask if the incident occurred during the summer on a Friday or Saturday night when beer drinking is common. Anyway, it appeared that I could reach the state park long before dark. I kept going, found the right road, and confidently headed for Lake Seminole State Park.

By mid-afternoon, I was again pedaling down the throat of a southwest wind. "Well," I consoled myself, "this is the last day going west. Tomorrow, I rest at the park. At least the road is flat and free of traffic." I reflected on my route thus far and found myself paraphrasing Sidney Lanier, Georgia's most quoted poet. Out of the hills of Rabun, down through the valleys of Lincoln, I hurried amain to reach the coast, then wandered through Marshes of Glynn, from St. Marys, Westward Ho!

Interrupted by a ferocious dog, I had to sprint on the bicycle and ended up spraying him with water. I learned from a breeder that dogs hate water. She splashes every squabble that occurs among the puppies in her kitchen. This animal must have been a hunting dog; it could run. I'm usually not concerned, unless they get their ruff up. This one growled, with shining teeth, but gave up easily after the water splash. I put the bottle away and concentrated on propelling the bicycle, leaving the dog well behind. Maybe he stopped at the end of his territory.

I continued on Spring Creek Road, also GA 254, but markers were infrequent. After crossing GA 310, passing crops and pigs, I entered Seminole County and returned to pine trees and flat, slightly rolling terrain. Then I passed a farm where there were rows of little, staked plants. From a distance, they looked like tomato plants. At the end of the field, several people were inserting stakes that a machine then air-hammered into the ground.

Even though the wind had freshened, as it does in the afternoon, I was barely making seven miles per hour on a slight downgrade. Both water bottles were empty, and I was feeling thirsty. I hoped the next intersection would have a store, and that soon I would arrive at the state park. There was a store, and I downed a V8 juice, quickly followed by a diet, decaffeinated Coke and some taco chips. The woman said the state park was only two miles away. Outside, I filled my two water bottles, and drank one. When I arrived at Site 12 in Seminole State Park, overlooking a lake inlet, it was shortly before 6:00 P.M. An hour later, my tent was up and I was clean and cool. I had sprayed my left leg with Solarcaine, and drunk two more bottles of water. A salad of lettuce and tuna fish made a fine supper. I had bought a large bag of bite-size donuts at the Flowers Bakery Outlet in Bainbridge, so dessert stretched until bedtime.

At twilight, after watching the light on the lake, I crawled into my tent and read the *History of Okefenokee Swamp*. Though I was very tired, today's 64 miles had brought me to the opposite corner of Georgia from Rabun County.

"I did it! I pedaled half-way around Georgia, the largest state east of the Mississippi River! I have earned a rest day!"

Wisteria House

Upstream

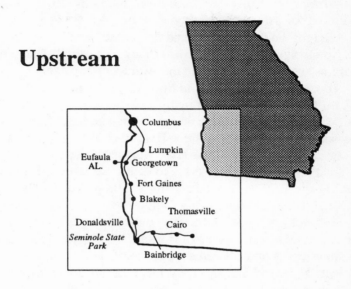

Seminole State Park Campground, Thursday, March 28

I do not recommend drinking little water during the day, and then a gallon or more before going to bed. I made quite a few moonlit trips to the bathhouse. On one sojourn I found an inch-long, pale-green frog eyeing me from the toilet seat. With one finger, I gently touched its rear and it hopped away. I saw the froglet several more times during the night, but by morning it was gone.

I remained in the tent until mid-morning, reading and eating a breakfast of banana and more donuts. Then I emerged for a time and watched a brown thrasher through my binoculars. Blending with the pine needles on the ground, it pulled and ate worms and other goodies. I showered, sprayed my sunburn, and threw all my clothes, except what I was wearing, in the washing machine. The wind was brisk, and my laundry was soon dry, hung from a length of parachute cord with small plastic clothes pins I carried in a nylon bag. Even my hands and arms were tired, so there was no doubt that I required this lay-about day.

History of Okefenokee Swamp, written in the 1920s and recently reprinted for sale at the park visitor's center, provided my reading material for the day. In it I found the phrase "wreck and ruin," which I have always heard and used as "rack and ruin." I also read that "saplins" refers to any pine in the swamp, of any age.

I dozed off and met a friend from Singapore in a dream, which was fun for I hadn't seen her for many years.

My mid-morning snack was miso soup and decaffeinated tea. At the washing machine, I met Irene Haj from New York, who invited me to come over to their trailer to chat. Her husband, Ed, told me they had decided not to work themselves to death. He retired from the police force at age 52. They turned over the bar they owned to their children, although they help out during football season. They travel in their trailer several months of the year, until home beckons them to their farm near ski country, south of Buffalo, New York. They had heard a weather report of a 50 percent chance of rain through the night. It looked like rain off and on all day, but none fell. Later in the afternoon, I watched a red-bellied woodpecker near my tent.

"I have no energy to do anything today. Why am I this tired? Is it because I ran out of my potassium supplement? Maybe it's because I got so dehydrated yesterday." I was angry that the man who had promised to send me another bottle of KM had failed to do so, and I tended to blame my energy shortfall on the lack of it. Repeated phone calls had resulted in assurances that it had already been sent, or that he didn't know where to send it, or some other excuse. I didn't know the real reason except that he had proved himself unreliable, and I should have had better sense than to count on him. Instead of dwelling on somebody else's broken promise, however, I wrote some postcards I had promised to send.

I adore just sitting and listening to the wind in the pines above. The cones were large here, and after dark, several campers made small fires of them, wrapping the evening in smoky pine aroma.

Seminole State Park Campground, Friday, March 29

A pair of Canada geese flew honking over the inlet, the campground, and the lake; more were feeding along the shore while I packed my tent in the morning. Motorboat fishermen had gone out, while others fished quietly from shore. When I left about 7:00 A.M., gray and white clouds were boiling overhead. A cool breeze blew and red-winged blackbirds announced "tick tick chit chit" from the under-brush. A red-bellied woodpecker flew overhead. I could hear blue jays yelling. I felt wonderful. I hadn't brought too much food with me and no one had fed me, so I'd eaten only what I'd had. Perhaps I lost a little, or at least avoided gaining, weight for one day.

During the mile of pedaling to get out of the park I debated whether or not to go to the office to pay. Several times I had offered to pay the ranger, but he didn't want to take the money and said he would get it later. He didn't. Finally, I decided I'd feel better and have a better day if I paid, so I did. I ended up in a long chat with three park officials, one of whom was the superintendent. He had just returned from a state park conference in north Georgia, and said they are going to limit the number of people who can come to crowded Vogel State Park.

In Georgia, and in many other states, you can take any number of people into a state park campground in a motor home or trailer camper, and usually can pitch one tent on the site, though vehicles are generally limited. Senior citizens and veterans receive discounts. Bicyclists, though, are permitted only two tents and four bicycles per site. If four bicyclists arrive, each with their own tent, they must pay twice as much as a motor home full of people pulling a car! Georgia should reconsider this policy. Sport bicycling is growing. So is the use of bicycles for transportation, because it's healthy for the rider and the environment. Inconsiderate fees discourage bicyclists from spending weekends or vacations visiting state parks, and could be interpreted as discriminatory.

I told the ranger about being turned away from a state park in New England after a long day of pedaling because it was full. All I needed were a safe place to put my tent and use of the bathhouse. I would have been happy to stay in the day-use area, at a picnic table, but the rangers said they could not make any concessions. I had to pedal an additional eight miles to a private camp.

The Georgia ranger responded, "That would not happen in Georgia. We wouldn't turn you away." I didn't argue, but I didn't believe a ranger would risk his job to benefit a stray bicyclist. What I said was, "Well, rules are rules. I didn't know rangers had that much latitude in Georgia."

I'd enjoyed Seminole. I pedaled out to the road, turned left, rolled a short distance and took a right turn onto GA 39. It would carry me to the Layside Bed and Breakfast in Blakely. The ranger had said I would be climbing hills for the entire north leg of the journey. Obviously, I'd be going upstream beside the Chattahoochee River. It had been tamed, since my childhood, by dams that created Lake Walter F. George between Fort Gaines and Columbus, and Lake West Point north of Columbus. Where the river turned inland, I would continue north. I've often been sorry that I never took a riverboat trip before the dams were built, while the river was navigable from the Gulf of Mexico to Columbus. The dam system included locks, so the trip is still possible by boat.

GA 39 was straight and rolling, each "up" a little steeper than the "down." Looking into the distance, I could see a gradual climb. But the "rollies" were gentle. I like rollies.

At a junction store, I bought grapefruit juice and a bag of Tom's Peanuts. The storekeeper told me a tornado was predicted, so I should be alert. It was an overcast day, with some very black clouds swirling overhead. Dust from freshly plowed fields swirled into dust devils or just blew in sheets, like rain. Happily, that same wind was pushing me forward.

I was delighted, for it was cool. I certainly did not need more sun for a few days. Meadowlarks and whippoorwills romped over the fields on the wind. Wisteria — climbing like kudzu up light poles, pine trees, bushes, homes, and fences — would have made beautiful slides. I wish I could have photographed the wisteria's fragrance; it too rode on the wind.

When I reached Donaldsonville it was drizzling and I was ready for breakfast. I looked up and down from the junction, then chose Lois' Restaurant, where I ate eggs, grits, and toast, and drank orange juice. After I'd eaten and paid, one of a group of men sitting at a table asked about my bicycle. At a lull in the questions, I waved and went outside. I thought the rain had stopped but it was still drizzling enough that I decided to go back in and eat a piece of egg custard pie. No sooner had I picked up a fork than the rain came down, harder than ever. It fell thickly, like water from an overturned bucket.

I ate the pie slowly, thinking of the lessons life in Singapore had taught me about tropical showers: the harder it rains, the sooner it quits; an umbrella is useless; if you go out, you get wet; when the air is warm, rain feels good.

It let up again. I headed for the door.

One of the men asked, "What do you do in the rain?"

"Eat too much." I laughed, then continued,"Get wet."

Someone else in the group mentioned that they came here to get their newspaper. "This table is our newspaper," he said.

Another added, "You'll find it the same in every small town in Georgia."

I responded, "You bet it is, and it's the same newspaper that serves every small town in America."

Another spokesman added, "There's another place with a table like this down the road, meeting at the same time."

A voice cut in, "Now, don't be critical."

"I didn't say one was better or worse, I said there was another."

I thought, "Yes, but he perceived your thought and I got the message, too." Clearly, neither group would be caught dead at the other's table, and they don't exactly swap news, but somehow, on the job, in the fields, when two pickup trucks block a road while drivers josh and laugh, the news gets around and will appear next day at the other table.

In smaller towns where there is only one cafe, different tables serve different groups. Talk passes among the tables, but occupants do not. Oh yes, they may stand and talk, as I did, but not sit down without an invitation. Strangers should observe carefully where to sit on entering a small place; at least I do. There are always places reserved, by custom, for the owner. There are "newspaper" tables. Women are seldom present, except perhaps at the owner's table. However, if a stranger takes a "reserved" table, its usual occupants will say nothing and convene at another table that day.

I asked about the fields of yellow flowers that appeared to be planted like a crop. One man said they were canola plants, which have a seed that makes oil without cholesterol, for salad and similar uses. "We grew sunflower seeds for oil in the past. This is the first year of trial for canola." He called my attention to the fact that wild mustard, growing along the road, is about the same color and looks similar.

It was still drizzling just before 10:00 A.M. but I headed out for Blakely, 24 miles ahead. It didn't take long to get there. I traveled with little effort and a fine tailwind, at 18 to 20 miles per hour. Along the way, I watched the cattle egrets. From the state park to Blakely, I'd pedaled 42 miles in about three hours, with several stops, including the long breakfast at Lois' Restaurant. Weather had ruled out going by way of Colquitt and Mayhaw, where the special mayhaw jelly I'd eaten in Darien is made.

Entering town I stopped at a junction to read the marker for Three Notch Trail. It was an important route from the early 1800s. It is believed that scouts for General Andrew Jackson's troops marked the route with three notches on trees as they proceeded toward Fort Scott to fight the Seminoles in Florida. The route had been an old Indian trail between Fort Gaines and Fort Scott, a horse or foot trail. Later, for early settlers, it was a wagon road that appeared on maps as early as 1820.

At the Blakely courthouse I saw the Confederate flagpole made in May, 1861, of a long-leaf pine tree that grew a mile away. It was hauled by oxen and erected where it now stands. It is the last original Confederate flag staff still standing in Georgia.

My attitude toward the Civil War is that the sooner people focus on the future and quit rubbing their noses in past discontent, the better for everyone. I'm pleased to note there has been considerable progress in this direction since I was a child in south Georgia. For this reason, combined with a genuine disinterest in "The War," I have made few references to it.

I left my stuff with Ted and Jeanneane Lay, at Layside Bed and Breakfast, and following their suggestion went off to the Steak House Restaurant for lunch. Then I rode to the Early County Court House square, pedaled around it, and headed for the Kolomoki Mounds State Historic Park. While reading signs on the peanut warehouses I heard a telltale "pssst," and put on the brakes as my tire went flat. I'd left all my panniers, including the bicycle pump, at Layside. Although I had another tube and the tire irons required to install it, Presta (French) valves cannot be pumped in a filling station. Fortunately, I had only a mile to walk to the bed and breakfast. The minute I reached the top step on the porch and began repairing the tire, the rain came down in torrents. I went in and visited with the Lays while the rain continued. When it stopped I decided to head out again for the Kolomoki site and museum; it was still early afternoon. My tailwind-aided ride, over rolling hills under a boiling black-and-white sky, was dry.

Exhibits at the site depict Indian history in the area from about 5,000 B.C. to the end of the Kolomoki period in the 13th century. I could hear thunder above and water pounding on the roof, and was doubly glad to stay inside. Though small, the museum is a jewel.

When the rain let up I went to see what is believed to be the largest Indian ceremonial center in southern Georgia. To me, the 56-foot, grassy clay mound resembled the stone mounds in Mexico. Few rocks are available in this area. It's believed there was once a population of 2,000 at the main village. Excavations suggest the first settlement was created about 800 A.D. by Indians who combined features of the Swift Creek and Weeden Island cultures that developed farther south. Several hundred years later these had evolved into the Kolomoki culture.

I wondered whether the mounds had been a platform for teachers. Did the shape symbolize bringing down the Word from above, as in other cultures in South America and Egypt? I also wondered whether use of the mounds as burial places came long after the disappearance of the teachers, along with much of their wisdom. After all, their teaching was not recorded. Indian laws and beliefs were handed down orally for centuries as were the teachings of Moses, Jesus, Buddha, and Krishna.

In our society, the value of oral teaching has been overrun by printing rollers and camera reels. A speaker can insinuate, inflect, and suggest, so that each listener can hear on a level supported by individual experience. Unfortunately, it wasn't until long after college that I learned a person cannot listen with care and take notes at the same time. While working at the CIA, I began to practice listening, first, then making notes soon afterward. It requires mentally separating the few essential points made from the many illustrative examples given to support them. If you can remember the points, you can supply new examples. This interest of mine grew to include all types of communication techniques. I still have to remind myself that a person can't listen and talk at the same time. I need more practice listening. Writing, of course, is the ultimate monologue!

It began to rain on my musing as I observed the great mound. The sky darkened again, all around the horizon. I needed to head for shelter —fast. I pedaled into the fiercest wind I'd encountered during this trip. Slowly, I inched my way seven miles to Blakely. Riding in the rain is not unpleasant as long as the cold fails to take hold. It had taken hold of me by the time I carried my bicycle up the front porch steps of Layside. A hot shower and dry clothes fixed that.

Ted and Jeanneane Lay, the owners of Layside, had spent many years in the military and in the Washington, D.C., area. Jeanneane grew up in Atlanta, so we found many zigs and zags of pleasant conversation.

They told me that Birdson, Blakely, and Singletary peanut companies used to dominate the town, but were now owned by a Virginia peanut conglomerate. Soybeans and cotton crops are expanding. Solutions to the boll weevil problems have been found, and machines are now able to provide much of the labor for cotton harvesting. Thus I understood why cotton has recently been getting so much marketing attention; production is becoming cheaper and more efficient.

I asked Ted if a pine tree can be identified by the size of its cones. "No," he replied, "size has to do with how much water the tree consumed. However, when you know enough, the cone, or seed, like the feather, will identify its host tree or bird." Cones in Seminole State Park were the biggest I'd seen, and I would have liked to have gathered a few to take home, as many other visitors were doing.

I enjoyed the company and conversation of the Lays, and felt right at home. Combining what I heard from them with what I had heard in other small towns, I got the impression that in the South one can identify whether people are Methodists or Baptists by which bank they use. People tend to trust the bank owned by a member of their congregation.

The Lays like the people of Blakely and have lived there a number of years. However, in retrospect, they thought they should have worked longer and not moved so quickly after retiring. We began talking of Army life in Japan and elsewhere. They told me about their four children, all with families, scattered all over America.

It was a wonderful, heartwarming visit. Before going to sleep, I thought about how little I'd heard about southwestern Georgia before this trip. I found it heaven for bicycling.

Blakely, Layside B&B, Saturday, March 30

Pleasant talk continued at breakfast, but I tore myself away from the fine company and rolled out of Blakely. I took College Avenue and Fort Gaines Road, then headed north on GA 39. I passed a number of shacks, and wondered how people could live that way. On one porch, four dogs slept; one raised its head and put it down as I went past.

I smelled the pulp mill that the Lays had said was ten miles away, but the fragrance of wisteria still dominated. As I rounded a curve it was replaced by the odor of natural gas, as I came upon a cross-country pipeline. So many pipes and metal boxes were humming above ground, I thought it might be a pumping station.

About three dozen goats, of various sizes and colors, grazed in a fenced pecan grove, and two pileated woodpeckers flew overhead about a mile apart. Then I came upon four vultures sitting on fence posts. Two more glided in. Three more, on the ground, were evidently feeding on a putrid deer carcass. They all left as I approached. The deer must have been hit by a car, then stumbled down the bank.

The road climbed slightly — a lovely road for biking. If I hadn't had a headwind, I really would have been moving. On this Saturday morning before Easter there were few cars; 14 the first ten minutes, ten the next. When I came to a slight downgrade I felt so good that I pedaled hard and got up to 12 miles per hour against the headwind. On longer grades, I reached over 14 miles per hour. Whenever I climbed a small rise, I could see a long way ahead.

After nine miles I entered Clay County, reputed to have more welfare cases than any other county in Georgia.

Going down to cross Kolomoki Creek, which is very swift, I got up to 25 miles per hour but I couldn't do more than five miles per hour going up the other side. The Kolomoki Indian site and mounds were located where this and two other creeks came together.

On the roadside grass, I noticed that someone had left behind the bottom piece of an auto jack. There would be trouble when the next flat occurred and the jack was useless.

Suddenly, I was in Fort Gaines; I had reached the junction of GA 37 and GA 39 (Washington and Hartford Streets). I got off the bike to read the marker, "Queen City of the Chattahoochee." Fort Gaines was called Highland Town by the Indians, until the frontier fort was established in 1816. As a steamboat shipping port for cotton brought from many miles on either side of the river, it grew to become the most important stop between Apalachicola and Columbus until the railroads came in 1858. On the bluff traces still exist of a slide for propelling cotton bales into warehouses along the river.

As I moved about the town other markers told me that the fort contained two blockhouses, guarding a 100-square-foot area, enclosed by an eight-foot stockade. I wasn't certain where the original fort stood or where I should go to see whatever was still there. I had a package to mail so I headed down Hartford Road, which remains the main street. I passed the Spur gas station and chuckled at its sign: "Chili Dogs and Anti-Freeze."

After a long wait in line I emerged and saw a woman coming out of a restaurant across the street. She was carrying a styrofoam container. I asked if the food was good, and she replied, "Oh yes."

I wasn't hungry yet, though, so I asked a man where the old fort was. I would have headed toward the river. He directed me down the main street, to a church where I should turn. "Then go to Bluff Street and follow it," he said, "and you'll run all over it." One old fort blockhouse stood on the bluff. The view allowed me to see far into Alabama, and offered a full view of a crook in the river. Nothing could stir on that river that a lookout wouldn't see. The blockhouse, which leaned to one side, was reconstructed of logs. It was perhaps eight feet square on the bottom, and ten feet square on the second story. Below, houses of the period had been reassembled. I thought the smallest might be a privy but I looked inside and it was about six feet by seven feet with no windows, a full floor, and one door. Another house had two rooms. The largest house had several rooms connected by a "dog trot" open space, perhaps the origin of a modern breezeway.

While I was looking at these houses, three men scrambled up the bank from the highway below and exclaimed excitedly over the log houses of the village. Tom Barthel and his son Jeff had come from Illinois the day before to celebrate older son TJ's honor student graduation from the School of Army Aviation at Fort Rucker. They were on a sightseeing lark before going home for Easter. TJ had learned how to fly helicopters as his National Guard assignment for the Persian Gulf War. Now 25, he was going home to continue National Guard service part time, and find a pilot's job. I asked if he would have to compete with pilots returning from the war who had combat experience.

"No," he grinned, "they are regulars and will stay in the military longer. I just go home now and I'm free and trained."

"Are you sorry you didn't get there in time to participate?" He shook his head. "Then I guess you came out of the war pretty well," I observed.

"Smelling like a spring rose."

We all laughed, took photos of each other, and shook hands all around. I gave him some suggestions about getting into bicycling at home because he thought running was getting too tough on his knees and legs.

I pushed my bike to a revetted old cannon from the Civil War and read that it commanded the river for two miles downstream but was never used.

Overflow prisoners from Andersonville had been kept at Fort Gaines, which also served as a hospital. The town was named for General Edmund Pendleton Gaines, born in Virginia in 1777, the son of a Revolutionary soldier. He was related to five U.S. presidents who served during his lifetime. He built the military highway between Nashville, Tennessee, and Natchez, Mississippi. In 1807, he arrested Aaron Burr and testified at the trial. Although Burr was acquitted, his distinguished political career continued to be tainted by rumors. Gaines fought the British in 1814 at Fort Erie. He also fought in the Seminole and Creek wars, as well as in the Mexican War. He was an advocate of military highways and steamboat transportation. I made a mental note to ask Courtney if her husband might be related to Gaines.

I pedaled the few blocks to the restaurant but went past it to look at the Coca-Cola sign on the side of a building. I had seen it on my way into town. It had to be quite old, or a replica, for it contained the words "relieves fatigue" and a large "5ȼ." I was pretty sure Coca-Cola hadn't used "relieves fatigue" in its advertising since coca was removed from the formula. The red color of the sign was curiously dull, almost a brick color, instead of the vibrant, brilliant red we are accustomed to seeing. Yet the sign looked complete and newly painted. Perhaps it was painted to look old.

I was hungry. I would photograph the sign later. After ordering at the counter I watched the people while waiting for my lunch. The black men who had occupied two booths left. I sat in one them. The other two booths, by the windows on the main street, were filled with eight white women, chatting. A young girl, waiting for someone who finally came, perhaps her father, talked with the women. There was another room of tables, but it was empty. The women workers, both black and white, joked among themselves and with customers around the room as they prepared the food. I felt invisible. Everyone seemed to know each other. A woman in paint-spattered jeans and a sweatshirt came in. She also knew everyone. She ordered, then went looking for an ashtray. By this time, three booths were empty, but the only ashtray was on mine. I said, "There's one here," and handed it to her. She took it and returned to the counter.

I still felt invisible, though of course everyone knew I was there. It is a great mistake to think people in a small town are unobservant or dumb.

I was getting quite hungry, so I walked over to the counter again. One of the workers had placed some iced tea on a tray and was heaping a plate that looked like my order. I drank half the tea, and she filled it up after handing me the rest of my meal. I was about to sit down again, when the woman with the cigarette asked, "Is that your bicycle?"

"Yes," I replied and sat down to eat. When she got her food, she asked if she could join me. She began plying me with questions about where I was from and where I was going. Everyone listened to my answers. Though I paid more attention to the catfish on my plate than the woman, she kept asking questions. To get her talking while I ate lunch, I asked, "What do you do?"

She said she was a carpenter and sign painter.

"Oh, good. Then I can ask you about the Coca-Cola sign. Is there some special significance to that odd red color?"

Aggie Ferguson told me she and her partner had restored it. I just ate and listened, fascinated, as she recounted the story. The project took two weeks, and led to commissions to restore the oldest sign ever found, on a building in Cartersville, and a sign on a drugstore in Atlanta. The Cartersville sign was from 1894 and had been found under 22 coats of paint! Its restoration resulted in a story by CNN aired on the world wire, five times a day, for a week. Aggie didn't know how wide the distribution of CNN was until she received a letter from a friend who had seen her, and the sign, on TV in Finland.

It all started in Fort Gaines. Jimmy Coleman, Chair of the Clay County Economic Development Council, Mrs. Virginia McAllister

Hall, and Mrs. Edwina Arnold Gardner, whose husbands worked many years for the Coca-Cola Company, wanted to restore the old sign on the brick wall of the Mills Building. The building became visible from the major highway junction when the church next door took down a building to create more parking. The women arranged private funding; Jimmy Coleman okayed the restoration and functioned as advisor. The Coca-Cola Company no longer puts signs on brick buildings, and did not fund the project. Other than providing encouragement and research facilities, the company did not participate. It sounded to me as though Mrs. Hall was the major financial backer and the motivational spirit of the project. Her late husband, "Red" Hall, had been a goodwill ambassador for Coca-Cola. He'd had the Coca-Cola sign in his hometown of Newton, Georgia, restored several years earlier. As a memorial to him, Mrs. Hall wanted to fulfill his dream to provide an attraction for tourists to Fort Gaines. The small committee found and hired Allison Free and Aggie Ferguson, artists from Lexington, Georgia. Aggie described how the fatigue of hours of work in high temperatures was washed away by the friendliness of the people of Ft. Gaines. "An hour seldom passed without someone bringing us a cold drink or asking questions or just standing to watch us work. It was long and hard, chipping layer after layer of paint. Everything we needed and had not brought was provided by someone — more water hose, an extension cord, ladders, a chair, umbrella for shade, and constant interest and friendliness. I fell in love with the town completely. That is why I moved here."

Also, Aggie confirmed that Clay County has more people on welfare than any other county in Georgia. She said some people want to be on welfare, and know all the tricks to stay on it. She described a lady who at age 51 got worried because on his next birthday her son would go off food stamps and she wouldn't get them any more. So she got pregnant.

"How could this be changed?" I wondered. Aggie thought a while, then replied, "The government could refuse to give food stamps for more than a certain number of children, say three, no matter how many the family has." We went on chewing and talking about how to implement such a plan.

When we went outside after lunch the headwind was strong, and I asked about where to stay. It being Saturday I didn't want to stay on

the roads too late. I'd spent a lot of time at Fort Gaines and didn't expect to get beyond Georgetown. Aggie said Eufaula, Alabama, was interesting, and there was a Holiday Inn at the other end of the causeway across the river.

She had to go back to work and I had to pedal on, but she agreed to walk over to the sign with me for photographs. Before we parted Aggie told me she would send me clippings about the Fort Gaines restoration project.

I rode out of town about 1:30 P.M. With the headwind it would take me at least two hours to reach Georgetown. The day was cool and pleasant and I enjoyed the ride — what did speed matter?

It had been a big lunch, and I was feeling sleepy, so I pedaled past the Walter F. George Visitors Center, watching a pair of bluebirds as I went. A man on the roadside checking the boat he was towing told me the fish must know a weather change was predicted, because they weren't biting. A few miles further there were people fishing every-where, in boats and on the causeway-type bridge.

I went into a store and drank a V8. The toilet was stopped up so I pedaled up the road until I found a path into the woods and used the "roadside" facilities. After 23 miles, I entered Quitman County. Further on, I stopped to watch a hawk circling, the sun shining through its feathers, until it was out of sight.

Georgetown was established in 1833, a hundred years after Savan-nah. Originally called Eufaula, it was renamed in 1836 in honor of

Georgetown in the District of Columbia. As a Lower Creek Indian town, Eufaula was visited and described in 1799 by Benjamin Hawkins, a U.S. Indian agent. Eufaula was on the Georgia side of the Chattahoochee River, very near Georgetown's present site.

Changes in the area are a source of confusion for some people. Chattahoochee River water was legally in Georgia until it was dammed to make Lake Walter F. George. Then the river widened to a lake so its waters spread into Alabama, where a town called Eufaula is located. In an effort to attract more tourists to Alabama, Lake Walter F. George is known there as Lake Eufaula. I found one tourist handout that referred to Lake George/Eufaula.

For several moments I stood by a campground on the Georgia side, indecisive about whether I wanted to camp for the night or go to the Holiday Inn I could see on the other side. All afternoon Aggie's suggestion that the Holiday Inn was handy had been building a disinclination to camp. I would pedal over the causeway, look around, and perhaps give myself an Easter present of a night at the Holiday Inn. Besides, I'd had such a full, interesting day I wanted to relax and type in comfort, and perhaps watch some sports on TV.

I expected to be put off by the Holiday Inn price, but the clerk gave me a discount for being a member of the American Association of Retired Persons, in spite of my not being able to find my card. By 4:30 P.M., I was taking the panniers off my bike and had turned on the golf match — led by Fuzzy Zeller, Paul Anzinger, and Tom Watson. Later, I went to find a store for Sunday snacks and to see the lay of the land.

The Bluff City Inn (built in 1885, to replace the old Central Hotel that had burned) has been restored, with stores at street level and hotel rooms above. The old barber shop is still in operation. North of my motel were the homes of Eufaula, but the sign for McDonald's pointed the other way. I was sure to find a grocery near it. I did, and returned to the motel room with a half-gallon of grapefruit juice, a box of Grape Nuts, three yogurts, a bag of Smartfood popcorn, a box of rye Triskets — and a burning interest in several couch-potato-TV hours.

I flipped on the tube and stretched out on the bed long enough to be sure I would never move again — even to get ice. Then the phone rang. It was Aggie, who had driven to find me after she finished work.

Apparently there wasn't much to do in Fort Gaines after hours; she had joked in the restaurant about working eight days a week. I could identify with that — I'd worked extra time for 30 years to ward off loneliness. While waiting for her to come from the front desk to my room, I realized I was lonely now; I was glad she'd come.

Aggie got me laughing as she recounted her search through every campground on the way to Eufaula. Even with all the stops looking for me, it took her no more than an hour. I had pedaled less than 25 miles since leaving Ft. Gaines. She suggested driving around Eufaula in her truck to see the historic houses before it got dark, then I could go back and look again in the morning. We set off in her pickup, roaming up and down the streets. I asked if any of the small, derelict frame houses I'd seen in the country were built of heart pine. Some were; a friend of hers bought and disassembled them and sold the wood.

We prowled around a wonderful large house on West Broad Street, the Kendall Manor, started in 1858 and completed in 1864. It had a "For Sale" shingle hanging out, and was run down and empty. From the porch we looked through 14-foot windows that didn't reach the ceiling. They had the largest nine light panes I'd ever seen. Aggie thought the room ceilings might be 24 feet high. Many of the windows were covered by blinds, but we looked in wherever we could. The house had been added onto at the back. We found a ladder to the addition roof, from which we could look into the second floor of the main house. There was no furniture but there were large, cheap Pakistani-type rugs. Indications of neglect and abuse made me wonder who had occupied it. Repairs, especially the roof, had been done carelessly. The roof had obviously leaked but efforts to put on new tar were so bad it would probably have to be completely torn off and rebuilt. There was severe water damage, partially concealed in places under the eaves. There wasn't much paint on the house, so scraping and painting it wouldn't be such a bad job, Aggie decided. The porch columns, however, were wooden and fluted, and there was detail around the front door that would require time to restore.

Overall, the exterior wasn't bad except for the roof. Even the new shingles had been of poor quality and did not appear to have been put up well. The house was sound and we spent our time there discussing how to restore it to its former status as a leading Eufaula residence. Talk is cheap, though. Climbing down the ladder, we decided it would be a poor investment unless a person had a lot of money for restoration.

Aggie bought a carry-out salad and we returned to my room and ate. Dessert was yogurt with Grape Nuts, washed down with iced grapefruit juice. I learned more about Aggie's sign restoration projects, and how she and her partner, Allison, had thought of starting a practical restoration school in Fort Gaines. Apparently, colleges now give degrees in restoration, but the work is all theory. Professionals in the trade have been disappointed in the impractical suggestions made by newly graduated students. Aggie and Allison had plans and economic backing lined up for the project — then Allison had a bad accident and the project stalled. I suggested that Aggie contact the SCAD (Savannah College of Art and Design) and propose a joint, practical venture. She said she would but Allison had been the organizer, and she couldn't work at present.

We never seemed to run out of talk, but when my eyelids began to droop, Aggie departed. I showered at last and typed notes for another two hours before ending a long day well after midnight.

Eufaula, Alabama, Holiday Inn, Easter Sunday, March 31

Up at 7:00 A.M., I typed notes again until 10:00, when I went to breakfast. It was a fine day, and I kept an eye on the clock, so I could spend time pedaling around to photograph the homes without carrying the panniers. If I returned to the room before checkout, I would have the whole afternoon to travel 23 miles, via the short route, or 40 miles on my preferred route along the river valley ridge to reach Lumpkin-Westville.

Reviewing the night before, I was reminded of how interesting any subject is when the person involved is enthusiastic and committed. After all, restoring Coca-Cola signs is an awful lot of painstaking, detailed paint-scraping. Imagine taking 22 layers of paint off a brick wall! (No crazier perhaps, than pedaling around Georgia.)

Eufaula was lovely. The dogwood trees were in full bloom, and the gardens were perfect. A tour of historic Alabama homes was scheduled for the next weekend, but I could enter some homes, if I stayed a few more hours. Just as I was adding Eufaula's historic homes tour to my "come back" list, I realized I had an extra hour to sightsee. I'd forgotten that the timeline follows the Alabama state line. My watch remained on Georgia time, so checkout was an hour later than my watch indicated!

At noon Georgia time I began to roll, fully reloaded, from Alabama, over the channel bridge and the causeway across Lake George/Eufaula. Going up the other side, I was welcomed by the old Georgia "State of Adventure" sign rather than the new slogan, "Georgia on My Mind." The bluff seemed lower on the Georgia side. I noted that since this part of Georgia wasn't burned during the Civil War, a variety of older homes remained.

On the outskirts of Georgetown I came to the junction where I had to choose my route. I took GA 39, the longer route closer to the river, via Florence and Providence Canyon State Park, instead of the direct route to Lumpkin. It continued along a ridge overlooking the river valley as it had south of Georgetown. Farmland filled the valley and pine trees covered the ridge. Where tree cutting had occurred and the replanted trees had not grown too high, I had a fine view as I pedaled.

Houses in the valley were built on the same design, two front doors and a porch across the front. Some had extensions at the back. They were built of wood and a couple of feet off the ground, resting on brick, stone, or blocks of wood. Each had a chimney at the center, or one at each end of the house, and each was covered by a steeply pitched tin roof. I'd lived in a slightly better, town version of this design as a child. There were better brick houses, too, on the W. C. Bradley Farm. I remembered Bradley as one of the distinguished families in the Columbus area. They have probably owned river valley land in this area for years and years.

A marker noted the former location of Roanoke, originally an Indian village. Incorporated in 1832, it held thirty families, a post office, and several stores. Roanoke was a thriving white settlement until attacked by a small band of Creek Indians in 1836. Repulsed at first by the townsfolk, two nights later some 300 Creeks returned and burned the town. It was never rebuilt. People who had sought refuge in a blockhouse then built Florence a few miles north, though first it was called Liverpool.

I also read about the Oconee Village, located a bit further north of my route near Omaha on the old Post Road (a GA 39 extension). The Oconee Indians lived there from 1715 to 1799. Their chief signed the treaty with General Oglethorpe at Coweta in 1739. Some years after many of their warriors fled to Florida, they became known as the Seminoles (runaways or outlaws), and formed the nucleus of the Seminole tribe. In the Seminole Wars, from 1817 to 1836, they fought Georgian settlers throughout the South.

At Florence I turned away from the river and headed due east, on connector GA 39 toward Lumpkin. I didn't realize until later that the turn had given me a tailwind. Going with the wind, as in sailing, is a lot warmer and you don't feel the wind as you do at other angles.

I stopped at Providence Canyon State Park. The canyons were formed by erosion, said to be caused by trickles of water that followed old Indian paths. They are often called "Little Grand Canyon" because of the brilliant colors from 43 different soils revealed in the canyon walls. The largest canyon is half a mile long, 300 feet wide, and 150 feet deep. They were named Providence for an old church which was moved out of the erosion path. The largest canyons east of the Mississippi River, they are now a state conservation park with hiking, backpacking, and picnic areas. I would suggest bringing your bicycle — the roads are good and traffic is light. Loop rides would be interesting.

After watching the slide show and walking around the top edges of the canyons, I continued on toward Lumpkin. Overhead flew a red-tail hawk, with half its left wing feathers gone. Not far away two more red-tails were chased by a crow. I watched them for a time through the binoculars — after checking underfoot for ant hills. Further along the road I saw my first wild turkey of the trip. It walked nonchalantly across the road ahead of me, stopped in the underbrush, and looked over its shoulder as I pedaled by. Seconds later, I heard a distant gun. Now how did that turkey know I wasn't hunting?

There had been a marker as I left the canyons noting that David Walker Lowe, a circuit rider, had built a house which turned out to be between two parts of the canyon. My mother's mother had been a Lowe from Lumpkin. The family moved to Atlanta when she was quite young, but grandmother often told my mother stories about the family and her life in Lumpkin' where her father had owned a store. Apparently, people trusted him to keep their money in the store safe before Lumpkin had a bank.

When I came to a junction I was in the residential part of Lumpkin and didn't know which way to go to get to the courthouse in Westville. A few blocks left, the road descended and I didn't feel like hauling my heap up any more hills. So I turned the other way where a blinker indicated a fairly large junction. At the quick-food place on the corner there was a car with two bicycles on top. As I approached, two men waved, their hands full of drinks and snacks. They were wearing bright bicycle jerseys. I stopped to meet Milton Brooks, a farmer from Newton, and Hank Harris, who did some bike racing. They had just completed a 49-mile loop ride. While eating pretzels we talked about bicycling equipment, routes, training, and their ride. Milton told me how to spell "canola," the yellow flowered crop I'd seen south of Donaldsonville. His opinion was it wouldn't amount to much, and farmers probably wouldn't grow it a second year. They headed home and I followed their directions to Michele's Restaurant and Motel.

At the post office I turned down a short street and saw the motel at the other end and a man and woman walking nearby. He politely asked where I was going. "Right here, to this motel." I'd had too little sleep last night and many hills since leaving the river ridge and I was hungry. They wanted to know where I had come from and so on. I was anxious to get off the bicycle and gave rather short answers. Before they proceeded on their walk the man said, "We live in that house, right there. When you get settled, come and have a drink with us. Come to the door where the cars are parked, in about an hour."

"Thanks, I will."

"Our name is Singer. See you soon."

At Michele's Restaurant and Motel, following Mr. Singer's suggestion, I entered the restaurant kitchen door. The cook assured me that I wouldn't want a room because the rugs were torn up, the furniture was moved out, and there was nothing to rent.

I pleaded with her, saying that I was traveling by bicycle, it was already cold, and while I had camping equipment, I had no interest in sleeping outside. (I thought the camp near Westville was six to eight miles away.)

"Could I please just camp in one of the empty rooms?"

Finally, she said she would look at the condition of one room. My hopes grew that I could get the room for half-price. I sleep in my sleeping bag, anyway, in motels for they seldom have blankets warm enough for me. With the waitress's help, the cook decided that I could have the room. The owners' children had been playing in there, so she had to clean up the toys and make the bed. As they requested, I sat in the restaurant and waited but not patiently. They had warned me it was not very clean, but I had not expected roaches and no hot water, and I had to pay the full $20 price! Nevertheless, I took a shivery shower, and to defray the evening cool put on the sweatsuit I used for pajamas. I stowed my things and the bike, and went to visit the Singers.

Sam and Ann Singer pulled out two volumes of Stewart County history in an effort to answer questions about my grandmother, Ada Lowe. We found references to my great-grandparents, and talked about where we went to school and where we lived. Sam Singer, who owned many properties, had spent his life in community work and local politics. Ann, originally from Americus, had worked hard in garden clubs and community restoration projects. We knew many of the same people.

They told me about going to Washington with Jimmy Carter's Peanut Brigade. I recounted how proud I was to claim I was from Georgia, although I knew none of the Carter administration migrants. As a civil servant I had served every president from Eisenhower through Reagan, and was an admirer of President Bush. I had never discussed politics or participated in party politics while working for our country; civil servants were not permitted to do so.

Sam Singer told wonderful stories about politics at the county level, which helped me understand better how our country really functions. Having spent my adulthood in the District of Columbia, I never considered counties — we have none — and knew nothing about "grass roots" politics in America.

I had come to understand some things about human motivation, and how politicians behave; those things are universal. I had never known how these universals applied in Georgia. Sam enlightened me with examples from his own experience. He told me about an editorial in the Atlanta paper (written by an editor who was not supportive of Carter), entitled "Jimmy Who." Some time later Sam was standing next to the editor during a Carter campaign speech. After being introduced, Jimmy said, "I'm Jimmy Who!" It brought down the house, and turned a disparaging editorial into a campaign slogan that caught on nationwide. It was a new twist on the old idea of rising from a log cabin to the White House, or from nobody to President of the United States.

I forgot about manners or time. The Singers graciously asked me to stay for supper. Ann offered to take me through the Bedingfield Inn the next day, and tell me about Lumpkin. She invited me to spend the next night in their spare bedroom. I really enjoyed their company and was thrilled to accept.

Lumpkin, Monday, April 1

In the morning I typed for a couple of hours, ate breakfast at the restaurant, then bicycled to Westville, arriving about half an hour after the historic village opened. That's when I discovered I was wrong last night. It was only one mile downhill instead of the six-plus miles I expected. The camp was on the far side of the village; it would have been fine there, except that last night was especially cool.

Westville village was created with real homes of the antebellum period, moved to recreate an 1850 Georgia town as an educational museum. I parked my bicycle and walked toward the Randle-Morton Store, originally built in Webster County. The nailheads in the shutters and doors were an old method of preventing thieves from sawing in to rob an isolated store. I had stepped into 1850s Georgia.

I bought a ticket and looked around at the gift items and books about pre-Civil War Georgia. Then I entered the village itself via the Singer Gates. They are a replica of gates to the old state capital grounds at Milledgeville, the most famous landmark in Georgia during the mid-1800s. Both the gates and the land on which Westville is built were donated by the Singer family of Lumpkin.

Naturally, I visited the comfort station first, grateful that its period exterior housed modern facilities. Smoke was coming from the chimney of the Grimes-Feagin House, so I went there. It felt so much like a home that it was hard to enter without knocking. I was met by Inez, who told me about the house being built in 1842 by Grimes for his son-in-law Feagin. It was a typical, middle-class family home. A suit of clothes made of handspun cloth, to be worn for Lafayette's visit, was visible. There was no problem about photographing inside or outside. Many historic homes forbid inside photos; Westville provides an opportunity to make a more complete record of your visit.

Across the street the double kitchen of the McDonald house had fireplace-cooking on one side, and the "newer" woodstove methods on the other. I was drawn to the woodstove by the scent of baking gingerbread' which I bought and ate with lemonade. I wandered through the upper-class home. Not far away were the cabinet shop and the shoemaker's shop, filled with tools and products of the day. The Singer House, also nearby, had another fireplace working. The whole town had a lovely aroma and feel. It was so much cooler inside the houses than outside, one could understand how people lived happily without air conditioning.

Getting away from large, air-conditioned buildings was one of the great attractions of retirement for me. They were so cold my joints ached, even in summer. The percentage of fresh air pumped through the system hourly was so small that my contact lenses burned my eyes, and if I failed to walk outside at lunch I had to drink too much coffee just to stay awake in the afternoon. Perhaps someday the American public will learn that air conditioning is unhealthy. Recirculated air, combined with fumes from photo laboratories, computer rooms, and cafeteria kitchens just might contribute to respiratory complaints. The human body is remarkable; if you give it time, it can adjust to almost any climate. Jumping from one air-conditioned space to another — office building to apartment to car — just doesn't give it a chance to do that. I gave up trying to change the world long ago, but I do believe each individual's job is to instruct and care for himself mentally, to ensure growth in a beneficial, ethical direction. I think of life as a marvelous do-it-yourself program! We lose balance when we look elsewhere for solutions to problems we created for ourselves. If we admit we caused them, then obviously we can fix them, and in less time, too. For me, this line of thought underscores the importance of attitude: a problem is often an opportunity in disguise.

I next came to the Patterson-Marrett Farmhouse. The log, dog-trot house was typical of farmhouses scattered across the countryside. A traveler's room to the right of the front porch was always left unlocked. I'd come across a similar custom while walking in the mountains of Nepal. There people expected travelers to sleep on the floor in front of the fire along with the family, friends, and relatives from other villages.

In 1850, Georgia farm families were isolated. They made just about everything they needed. Money was scarce, roads were unpaved, and travel was usually on foot or by horse. It amused me no end that the League of American Wheelmen, a hundred-year-old bicycle advocacy association, was lobbying for smoother, paved roads before Mr. Ford popularized the automobile. Now, bicyclists fight for the use of these roads.

At the back of the farmhouse, overlooking a plowed field, Louise Crocker was making sausage biscuits at an open fireplace. I was hungry again, so I bought one and asked if I could sit down in one of her chairs while eating. She also served coffee and lemonade. I asked if they grew crops in the field behind the house. "Oh, yes, sugar cane." she replied.

"Is it that dark purple cane?" I asked.

"It is," she confirmed.

"Do you ever chew it?"

"My husband plants cane for me and in the evening I sits on the porch and chews my cane. I truly like to chew cane."

"I remember when I was a kid, I was permitted to have a knife to cut cane to chew. I adored it. Is it as sweet and juicy as I remember?"

"Oh yes," Louise told me. She was a tall, jolly woman. She reminded me of Clara, who took care of me when I was small. I had watched Clara prepare food, and followed her around while she cleaned the house. Then, while she sat on the porch swing and shelled peas I listened to her stories about the "bug" (numbers-lottery) house in Phenix City.

I took another bite of sausage biscuit and it was gone. Louise and I continued to sit on opposite sides of the fireplace. Occasionally, she got up and looked in a pot. I drank some lemonade and asked about the fig tree outside.

"Do you get good figs off that tree over there?"

"They's small, sweet, good."

I took another swig of lemonade, and drifted into a memory of my childhood in Columbus. Our fig tree had been so old and large that at seven or eight, I could climb up and sit on the branches to get the ripe figs. The birds ate the figs at the top; the ants savored the figs on the ground, or climbed to the lower branches; I got the figs in between. It was a fine arrangement. I'd often wondered since whether the small purple figs were as good as I remembered. The last time I went to Columbus, a large parking lot had replaced my house, the fig tree, the barn I'd climbed around in, the slate-lined, double-decked grave of my favorite cats, both houses next door to ours, and the homes of my friends down the block. What a disappointment! Across the road, where I had flown kites, were now homes with trees. Had the trees not been so large — they were slow-growing oaks — I would not have believed 50 years separated the memory and what I saw that day. The creek where I slid down the clay bank and looked for birds still ran behind the fine homes. But the whole of Columbus had seemed shrunken; the street grid and distances were smaller. I wondered whether, on this visit, it would appear normal sized.

Returning to Westville and the present, I asked Louise, "Did you have to learn to cook over an open fire to work here, or had you learned that when you were young?"

"We had a wood stove to cook on when I was growing, but my grandmother cooked over her fire and I had watched and learned, so it wasn't hard."

The woman who made the gingerbread had told me that she had learned to cook at home on a wood stove. "It isn't any different from an electric stove. It's just slow and you have to watch the cooking. But it gives a good flavor." She said it wasn't any trouble and she liked her job at Westville, where she had worked for several years. She was much younger than I, perhaps in her thirties. Even I could remember turning on gas heaters in winter, and lighting them with a match. In some rooms we had only the fireplace grates, and burned coal.

The day was sunny and springy and the dogwood was in bloom. Inside the houses, in the shade, it was chilly. The wood fires took off the chill, made the houses smell wonderful, and provided atmosphere and realism. It really did seem more like a town than a museum. There was a warmth, friendliness, and naturalness to the people. Granted, their speech wasn't historically accurate. (In Plymouth, Massachusetts, the crew on the *Mayflower* and the inhabitants of the recreated Plimoth Plantation learned old speech and even act unfamiliar with cameras.) Still, at Westville the people exuded manners and courtesy in keeping with the earlier period.

My cousin, Frank Schnell, first brought me to Westville before it was open to the public, when two or three of the houses were not yet positioned. On the same trip, he took me to a nearby Indian mound that he was excavating. I'd wanted to come back ever since. The visit was a great satisfaction on many levels. Though I was not ready to leave, Ann Singer had offered to show me around Lumpkin, so I walked fairly quickly through the rest of Westville, intending to return later.

On the way out, I met Gus Daniel, who was making baskets and washboards. He was cutting on a piece of white oak with a knife, preparing it for basket weaving. Now old, Gus is the only basket maker around. He had been working at Westville for seven years, but he wasn't teaching anyone anything, he was just making baskets. I'd seen them for sale in the store. Hanging on the wall of the house behind where he sat cleaning cane strips was a completely hand-carved washboard. Gus had made it, but didn't have the strength any more. It was an older type than the washboard I rememberd being sold at the store, with wood sides and a galvanized, corrugated scrubbing area. In my childhood, we often heard street bands, and one of the instruments was a washboard. Our washerwoman also used one, and we had one around the house, for Clara sometimes "rinched" out a few things.

When I reached Ann's house, we walked over to the Bedingfield Inn. It stands on a corner overlooking Lumpkin's courthouse square. It was built in 1836 as a stagecoach inn and private home. The floor plan and stairs, which separate the inn from the private quarters, were interesting. Its interior was enhanced by gifts of furniture, clothes, and household items from many local citizens who had made the Inn's restoration a community project.

Ann and I walked over to the Drug Store Museum. Someone had donated a whole drug store, including the labeled bottles of substances, display cases, tools, and items for sale. Ann lifted the lid on the cinnamon stick jar for us to smell. We enjoyed comparing notes on people we knew in Columbus, or who went to Randolph-Macon

Woman's College. We found we had many friends or acquaintances in common. She invited me to move my things into their home, and to be sure to return in time for supper. They made me feel like a long-time friend or member of the family.

I pedaled back to Westville village, but walking down its streets, I realized I was getting tired. I was running out of reserve. When I get that way, I just want to sit down and do nothing, so when I reached the cotton press and the cotton gin, I sat on the steps and just looked at them. I tried to figure how they worked and what they did. The fresh-picked cotton was dropped from above into a box containing the gin cylinders. With broom-like teeth, the cylinders combed the seeds out of the cotton. The seedless cotton (lint) then dropped, or was blown out, while the seeds were collected separately. The large wheel and gears, which operated the gin cylinders, were turned by mules walking in a circle under the building.

Funny that I never questioned how the cotton got from the pickers' bags (croker sacks) into 500-pound rectangular bales, wrapped and bound for shipping. Now I saw how it was done. One "house" at Westville is the cotton press. It's also powered by mules. The whole top of the building rotates; it looks like a roofed-over, extra-large version of a letter press. The animals walk around and around the building to crank the pressure tighter on the cotton, pressing air out of it and mashing it into a wood mold while it is covered and bound into a bale that can be transported by wagon, train, or ship. The ginning and baling was done near the fields to avoid transporting the seed, two-thirds of the picked cotton weight before ginning. The cotton gin was so important because one person's hands could only pick seeds out of about five pounds of lint per day. A small gin operated by two people could yield four to six pounds of lint per hour. But with power, such as the mules, 60-100 pounds of lint could be prepared per hour. No wonder the brokers in Augusta referred to cotton as "white gold," and we all know Eli Whitney made a major contribution to the cotton industry by inventing the gin.

Cotton, the most important of vegetable fibers, has made economic history beyond the South. It had a potent effect upon the progress and politics of the leading industrial nations. In England, it played a large role in the industrial revolution. In the United States it has been cultivated for so long that it is only with effort that one recalls the fact

Cotton Press, Westville

that the cotton plant is not indigenous to Georgia, or to the United States.

When I returned to the Singer home, I was exhausted. I took a shower and lay down, too tired to read. I revived after a time, and read all the free papers I'd picked up about Lumpkin and Westville. Then I began to look in the *History of Stewart County* volumes to find information for my mother about the Lowe family.

During supper Sam recounted more stories. One of them was about a complicated dispute over the Democratic primary in Quitman County which resulted in a judgment that all the counties in Georgia had to strike Jimmy Carter from the ballot. Two counties failed to comply, and the votes in those counties were so overwhelming that he was able to carry the state and get the nomination. Otherwise, he could not have run for president. I heard this story three times and still didn't have the political savvy to understand its complexity. The point seemed to be that a series of grass roots flukes helped Jimmy Carter become eligible to run for president. I already knew that many Georgians, especially from Atlanta, didn't support Carter for national office based on his actions as governor. Comments I have heard in Georgia and elsewhere, since he began his international work from the Carter Center, have been positive.

I felt fortunate indeed to have been temporarily adopted by the Singers. Before the evening ended, we discovered more common ground. My mother thought her grandfather had sold the family store to a Singer. Sam checked it out and explained which store it was on the square so that I could describe it to her.

Lumpkin, Tuesday, April 2

After a quick breakfast I said goodbye to Ann and Sam and pedaled along the Stagecoach Trail, a drive-by tour of Lumpkin's pre-1850 homes. Then I took US 27 and headed north for Columbus. Soon I reached Cusseta, named for Kasihta, "The Peace Town of the Lower Creeks." Kasihta, mentioned in the narrative of DeSoto's expedition in 1540, had been on the Chattahoochee River, but was burned. Cusseta was one of the oldest and most important Lower Creek towns. In the census of 1832-33, it had 1,918 residents.

The road through Cusseta took me back to the highway, and soon I was pedaling through the Fort Benning military reservation, an area that holds fond memories for me. On the old main post, west of my route, was the place where I had watched polo games on Sundays and played with the other kids. We watched paratroopers practice from the jump towers. Once, when we were running through the woods, real tanks chased us. During the early months of World War II, I attended entertainments for the troops with my parents. My father had escorted some of the performers. I collected an autograph book of signatures and experienced the allure of grease paint and footlights.

My wheels rolled toward Columbus. I stopped to read about the old Federal Road, Georgia's earliest vehicular route leading westward. It crossed Creek Indian country, from Macon to the Alabama River, north of Mobile. Permission to open this trace was granted by the Indians in 1805. It closely followed the well-known Indian Trading Path from Augusta to the Creek Indians. Lafayette traveled this way in 1825, on his way to Alabama. The old road long served as a route to the west for emigrants and the post. The sign underscored the fact that the Chattahoochee River area around Columbus had been a major junction for river and road travel in all directions.

After 29 miles of pedaling I entered Muscogee County. I had reached my childhood home! Not far along a Hardee's sprang up. I drank tea and ate a sandwich and french fries, drank more tea and iced water, and read two newspapers. Two hours later, I completed the trip through the outskirts of Columbus and, via Brown Avenue, arrived at Wynnton School, my old elementary school. Since I was early for an appointment with reporters, I pedaled around the neighborhood and along Stark Avenue, where Betty Spain Houseman used to live. We played together while our fathers played chess. Author Carson McCullers had lived across the street, though she was much older than I. People on the street remembered her, and I had heard how she annoyed the neighbors playing the piano all the time. She had first trained to be a concert pianist. On the sidewalk, I met Shirley Parker Mitchell, walking with her mother. She was in my cousin Frank Schnell's class in high school, and now lives in Jacksonville. Even large small towns are fun! I wandered down a few more streets and identified places I went trick or treating, dressed as a witch and carrying my very own black cat. Then I found Sue Smith's home without looking up the house number.

Across the street in front of Wynnton School, I leaned my bicycle against a cedar tree and looked at my watch. I was early. Sandra Okamoto, Arts and Leisure editor, was going to interview me for the *Columbus Ledger-Enquirer.* I lay down on the grass, and thought about how glad I was to be "home" after 50 years of vagabonding.

Hometown

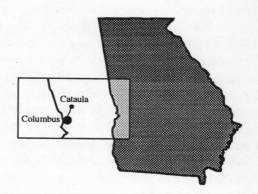

Columbus, Monday Afternoon, April 2

A car crunched on the drive. I didn't want to move. The door slammed. I sat up and opened my eyes. An attractive young woman was walking toward me. A tall man approached from a second car. That's how I met Sandra Okamoto from the Columbus newspaper, and Paul Logue from the Southwest Velo Club. Mike Haskey, photographer, soon came along, as did Jane Dillard Knight, a childhood and college friend, with her granddaughter, Marie. Doug Mote, a bicyclist, brought his camera. While we were talking at umpteen miles per hour, a commuter bicyclist, Bob Kirk, pedaled up on his way home. It was a joyous reception on the grounds of my elementary school.

Each of the men tried to lift my fully loaded bicycle; they found it possible, but difficult. Everyone, except me, wanted to know how much it weighed. I didn't care anymore because less than a block away was Sue Smith's house — and her car, into which I planned to put my stuff.

Sue and I were registered to attend a week-long Elderhostel — my first — in Rabun County, as soon as this trip ended. We would attend lectures on the settlement and history of the Appalachian people and gold mining in Georgia. I'd picked the time and the place so that I would have a firm deadline for the bicycle tour, plus a week of interesting diversions with people before I needed to sit down and begin organizing my notes about the Georgia tour. I was delighted that Sue could come because she is good company and fun. She would drive from Columbus and bring anything I left, including the packages I'd sent her from around the state. It would be great to have a friend visit my mountain house. It also gave me a way to return the favor. I would be staying with Sue this week, making her farm in nearby Cataula my headquarters. Frank Schnell and his family were out of town most of that time. Jane Knight had invited me, but her whole family had been sick, and I would see them anyway. It would be heaven to sleep in the same bed for a whole week!

The photographer had the pictures he wanted, I'd answered dozens of questions, and some of the people had left. Sandra, Bob, Kirk, and I remained as the rest scattered. Bob asked me another question about the tires on my bicycle, and I looked carefully at the rear tire. The tube was showing through a cut in the casing.

"Where is the nearest bicycle shop?" I asked him.

"Not far, a couple of miles, and I have to go that way on my way home. I'll show you."

I'd have to buy a tire at once, I explained to Sandra.

"Let some air out and you can get that far," Bob wisely advised. "I'll bet you came in on Brown Avenue. It has more glass than all the rest of Columbus put together!"

We laughed. I was thankful to have discovered the cut tire before it went flat. Bob waited while Sandra asked me a few more questions, then we waved her on and pedaled to Sue's house. I left the panniers and followed Bob across town to Mike's Bikes. I knew the road well. Many of the side streets were familiar and I longed to explore, but there was no time; without bike lights, I had to return before dark.

While taking off the old tire at Mike's Bikes, we found an additional cut. They installed a new tire for me in no time, in spite of being quite busy. While we waited, Bob Kirk repeated the directions for my return, not realizing I knew this area, which had once been a cow pasture. We had crossed the railroad tracks, near the entrance to a club where I played musical chairs at birthday parties with other children. I had ridden my bicycle on the through street we took, as well as most of the cross streets.

Sue had arrived by the time I got back to her mother's house. It was supper time, and I sat down with Sue and her mother, Bet Blackmar, to eat and visit.

Later, Sue and I put the bicycle and all the bags, bundles, and panniers into her car, and drove to her farm at Cataula, 20 miles from Columbus. I would cover that distance by bicycle at least once before the week was over, closing the gap on two wheels instead of four. I fully intended to bike the whole perimeter route.

When we were kids, my first visit to Sue's farm must have been in the fall, because I remember picking buckeyes off a tree. A couple of years ago, after her husband died, I visited again. Jane Knight and other mutual friends had helped us find each other. This time, Sue showed me to the same bed I had slept in then. I fell into it so fast, I may not even have turned on the light.

Cataula, Tuesday, April 3

When I awoke, Lady, Sue's black labrador, was sleeping by my bed. I considered it a compliment, for she usually slept in Sue's room, and Sue wasn't awake yet. The birds were, though. When Sue woke up, we had a breakfast of sausage, grits, toast, eggs, coffee, and fruit. While eating, she explained that someone had given her two thousand seedlings (two-year-old, nursery-grown Loblolly pines) because they had planted all they needed and felt it was too late to plant more. She had planted a few the day before, and since rain was predicted tonight and for the next few days, she felt that if we got the seedlings in the ground at once, it might not be too late after all. The loggers had finished their work, and today there was a man with a 'dozer, pushing the trash tree limbs out of the way so we could plant. Sue had warned me there was work to be done. I didn't mind as long as it wasn't pedaling.

We loaded tools, and seedlings in buckets, into the truck. Sue was dressed in long pants, tucked into knee-high workboots. I wore cotton shorts, my cycling tennis shoes, a T-shirt, and a borrowed sunshade hat. Lady jumped in, we grabbed our water bottles and lunch, and Sue drove the pickup down the road. She turned onto a red-clay farm road where we bumped along until we reached the logging area. There we met Richard Stinson. He and Sue discussed the day's work — clearing the rest of the trash wood and repairing the road so that water would drain properly and the pickup could get around. Most of my friends who talk about manual work mean a couple of hours, at most, weeding a garden. I had somehow gotten the impression that Sue's main job was to supervise the work of others, and that I would be sitting around in the fields or woods, watching whatever was happening. I had put my portable computer in the truck to finish writing up notes about yesterday. They were never written. The only thing the computer did was get sat on by the dog, which hurt neither of them.

Sue had told me she would teach me how to dibble. It didn't sound hard, but I didn't know what it was. It never occurred to me that we would be digging holes and planting trees all day. It wasn't until we came to a clearing and took the trees and tools out of the truck that it began to dawn on me we were going to plant them. The seedlings were tied together and stuck in buckets, and it didn't look like many.

With a cheery grin, Sue picked up a tool that looked like a skinny shovel with a heavy pipe handle. "This is a dibbler. Would you like the heavy one or the light one?"

"What do I do with it?"

She demonstrated, "You lift it overhead by the T-shaped handle, drop it as hard as you can so the metal, wedge-shaped point on the other end pierces the clay ground, stand on the foot bar like you would a shovel, to push the dibbler in, wobble it around to make a hole, and finally take it out. Then take an 18-inch seedling out of the water, stick it in the hole, stomp the dirt back over it — not too tight — pull it up a bit to straighten the tap root, and stomp again. You pace two steps and do it all over again."

Sue grinned, "Trees in the same row are two paces apart, rows are three paces apart. That's it." I did one. Not so bad. I tried another with the light dibbler and decided I liked the heavy one best.

"Well," Sue said, "I have to go over to the other field and mark a road with tape for Richard, and then I'll come back and help you. You'll hear the truck, as you can hear the 'dozer now; none of us are far away, except when we go by road in the truck." She started the truck, Lady jumped in, and they were gone.

I looked at the dibbler in my hand and paced two steps. It was sunny, quiet, and not very hot. A breeze blew. I didn't care about its direction, as long as it continued to make the pines purr. Pretty soon I looked up and realized I'd completed a whole row. Dibbling was fun! It required almost no effort by my legs or feet, and quite a bit of arm and hand control. I was outdoors! Dibbling was a perfect antidote to bicycling.

By the time Sue came back, I had decided I really liked dibbling the holes, but didn't like carrying a bag full of wet trees on my hip. I've always been more efficient doing one thing at a time. Aloud, I wondered whether she would be willing to try working together side by side, instead of each doing a parallel row. I would dibble the hole, and she would stick the tree in and stomp it down. Since Sue had planted trees many times, and dibbling wasn't her favorite part of the job, she was willing to try. So we did the next row, one behind the other, talking full tilt as we went. Sue claimed we made much better time, and that the work was easier. We continued that way for the rest of the day. Each of us avoided that portion of the job

dibbler & seedlings.

we least enjoyed. The only problem was that sometimes we got so interested in our conversation, the rows were a bit crooked. We blamed that on the stumps, stopped for lunch, then kept on until all the trees in the truck were gone — about 900. Well satisfied with ourselves, we went back to the farm.

As a reward, Sue taught me to drive the tractor, and I cut some grass. Sue has the first model of tractor Ford ever made. It still runs well, because she has learned the mechanical skills to keep it going. Satisfied with my tractor lesson, Sue said we would be working with it later in the week. Then we got on her Honda mini-bike and raced over the farm fields and bumps. We looked at a meadow of May apples in bloom, then walked down to the rain-swollen creek to see if we could drive the tractor across. To prevent erosion, Sue wanted to scrape the earth and plant grass on the bare places before more rain came, perhaps tomorrow. By 7:00 P.M., Sue was in the shower. I took a bath and came out clean, including my hair. We sat down to supper in rocking chairs, then gave a short squint at TV before falling asleep.

Cataula, Wednesday, April 3

The next morning, we looked at what the 'dozer had done and found that Richard Stinson had completed his work. The sun had dried some of the fields. In spots where it baked the red clay, I could hardly get the dibbler point into the earth. Each hole took a long time, and considerable effort. But just when I was ready to quit, I would reach a soft area and move on at good speed.

In the afternoon, I did a lot of personal errands, like running into the outskirts of Columbus to visit White's Book Store, to see owner Betty Bush. I had been a flower girl in her parents' wedding, and remembered them fondly. Her mother had given me violin lessons until we moved away. There was enough difference in our ages that neither Betty nor I remembered each other.

I picked up the trip photos from Wolf Camera and Video, then went over to Mostly Software to get pages of notes printed out of my computer. Sue would bring them to the mountains, and I'd have them to work from after our Elderhostel week at Covecrest was over.

In the evenings, throughout the week, I spent a lot of time on the telephone with family and friends who were helping keep my life at home on track. Dorothy Samson read mail to me and paid bills, while Carol Melillo managed my rental property. Sue telephoned her family too, but during daylight hours we worked and cruised around the farm. I was extremely happy, and never had time to write a single word while we hurried to get more trees in the ground before it rained. It was great exercise for my arms and back, neglected during long days of pedaling.

Cataula, Thursday-Friday, April 4&5

We planted trees all day Thursday. It rained heavily overnight, and we awoke Friday, happy for the trees. I was glad we had run out, and that the man Sue called hadn't yet brought any more! We had also planted 200 pounds of grass seed, to prevent erosion on the new roads through the woods. Rain continued during the morning, so we did quiet work for ourselves in the house. Sue worked on taxes. I tried to figure out where I stood with notes and letter writing. I also refined the details of the route for the rest of the tour.

As I read maps and talked with people, a plan began to shape itself. I would depart on Wednesday, April 10, and ride to LaGrange, where Diane and Earl Johnson would meet me. They would stay in a motel overnight, and Earl would ride with me on Thursday, while Diane drove back to work in Atlanta and returned later to meet us. Karen Horne, in Bremen, wanted to ride with me on Friday, if she could get free from work. Earl might also continue Friday, with Diane going by car. Cass and Steve Brady wanted to ride with me on a weekend, if we could work it out. It looked like the first night in LaGrange, second night in Bremen with the Hornes, then north, perhaps to Summerville.

Friday afternoon cleared, and Sue suggested a walk to plant some more grass seed. She gave me a pair of high rubber boots, and we drove the truck to the creek ford. The water was almost knee high. Carrying buckets of grass seed, we cautiously slid our feet across the natural rock surface of the creek bed. Sue's father had filled it in somewhat, with cement, when the water was low, but it was slimy underfoot, and the current was swift enough to knock us down if we misstepped. Slowly, we got over what the dog thoroughly enjoyed swimming through. Then we walked up the logging road, strewing grass seed on the damp clay banks. We also planted the areas where logging trucks had turned around. It didn't take long to run out of seed, and we returned to the house for supper. Meanwhile, the man Sue had called had delivered another two thousand trees. The ground was still soft from rain, so she would be able to dibble holes for the trees, on her own, with less effort.

Cataula, Saturday, April 6

The day I arrived in Columbus, Paul Logue invited me to participate in a time trial being held on Saturday by the Southwest Velo Club. Their route was near Sue's farm, and I had agreed to come. I had only done two time trials before, both the same ten-mile course, and I hadn't been able to break 20 miles per hour, missing it by less than a minute. Although this event was with a racing club, in a time trial you pedal against the clock. I have the only heavy bicycle frame, with heavy rims and 1 3/4-inch tires, so I had a fine excuse for a poor performance, if I needed one. I expected to be the only old lady. I turned out to be the only woman. I'd never tried a 24-mile course, either. All week, I looked forward to the day's challenge.

If I had pedaled the dozen miles to the time trial course, my unused legs would have warmed up, and I'd have been able to ride faster. But I got up late and spent too much time talking over breakfast. Since I had a long list of things to do after the bicycle event, Sue offered me her car for the day. She went off in the truck to plant more trees; I readied the bike, put it in the trunk, and drove to the time trial course.

Paul introduced me to his wife, Vickie. He said I looked rested since Monday. Doug Mote was there with his wife, Gail, and a lot of their friends from the Fairdinkum Bicycle Club in West Point. Mike, of Mike's Bikes, was there, too. He certainly hadn't expected to see that new tire roll a time trial. (It had a rough tread like a mountain bike tire.) The other 14 participants were young men, on fine racing bicycles, some with tires half the width and rolling resistance of mine.

We met at Ellerslie, where a marker announced the Wire Road, route of the first telegraph lines from Washington to New Orleans, via Columbus, completed in 1848. In those days, prominent visitors came from Milledgeville (the capital of Georgia then) along the Wire Road. We pedaled it east 12 miles, turned around an orange cone and the time checker, and pedaled back. We started one minute apart. Being the slowest, I started first. I was passed by every rider except two, and they all beat my time. But it didn't matter; the course was my favorite sort of rollies with a "silk sheets" surface. I'd forgotten that term, commonly used during the Bicycle Ride Across Georgia (BRAG). It means an extremely smooth road surface (although you can imagine what a gang of guys could come up with in puns and jokes).

Out on the course, I missed the 53-tooth chain wheel on my road bike. With it, I could really hammer the downhills to make up for slow climbing. Also, this touring bike had no aero bars to get me down out of the wind and keep me there. So I stayed on the drops, kept my head low, and turned the 50-tooth chain ring as fast as I possibly could. I tried to remember to turn the pedals from the hip, with flexible ankles, to use the whole leg, and to keep the rotations as fast as possible. The new, quasi-mountain-bike, knobby rear tire really zinged. It was fun to go really fast.

Actually, the course was a shade under 24 miles; two of us recorded 23.9, although the official distance was listed as 24.2 miles. In any case, my time worked out at 19.9 miles per hour for 1 hour, 21 minutes, and 53 seconds. I was surprised and delighted. But the challenge to exceed 20 miles per hour remained.

Doug Mote invited me to stay at their home when I got to LaGrange. I accepted. Since Gail would be away, I suggested that he join the Johnsons and me for supper, as my guest. It was a great plan, for we could use his house and phone to find each other in LaGrange.

Gail, who had been timekeeper, and several other officials prepared to ride the course while the rest of us stuffed our bikes into cars and trucks. Gail made my day by saying she was glad I'd done a good time; it gave her something to aim for. This bunch was fun. It felt great to be on the bicycle again. Originally, I had planned to pedal to Columbus, spend a whole day there wandering around on the bicycle, then pedal back. But to save time, I decided to "do" town in the car, spending more time with people and places, and less on wheels.

Downtown, trying to find where my grandfather's coverall and overall factory had been, I decided on the 1400 block of First Avenue. Later, my cousin confirmed the location. I went by the Swift Mill and the former Carnegie Library, which now appeared to be storage, or a garage, attached to the mill. The hills didn't look as high, and the town plan itself didn't seem as spread out as I remembered it. Houses I pictured as large seemed medium-sized.

Broad Street, with the splendid grass park running down its center all the way through town, was there. Some of the streets were still brick paved. Though the Bradley Theatre appeared long closed, I remembered attending the first movie shown there. I identified the corner building on 11th and Broadway where I had sat with my parents in a beauty parlor on the second floor to watch General George Patton and his tanks parade along Broadway before leaving for World War II training. Mentally, I could hear the tanks now and see Patton standing in his tank with the shiniest helmet of the whole parade. The soldiers sat with stiff spines, arms folded in front of them, filling the backs of trucks.

On opposite corners of that intersection there had been Kresses and Silvers, ten-cent stores. Silvers was now a Payless Shoes; Kresses had become HL Green. It was in this area that I felt like I was in a scene from Carson McCullers' *The Heart Is a Lonely Hunter*. Although she was writing about Columbus when I was three years old, many of her descriptions were of places I remember from about the age of eight.

The old red brick courthouse was torn down and replaced by a fine high-rise building and garages, filled with police cars. Gone was the beautiful, landscaped courthouse square, with fountains and wonderful cannon at the corners, overseen by a Victorian red brick house of judgment.

My grandmother's house still stands between what was the Fort's home and the Albright's home, although they moved to the suburbs when I was still attending Wynnton Elementary School.

I was sorry that downtown seemed less prosperous than it had on my last visit, five years ago. The stadium at the end of town, where I watched my first football games, now looked very small. The house of my aunts Mimi and Fanny, where they made world-famous candy, was moved to lower Broad in the historic district. I remembered sitting in the kitchen, licking fudge spoons, and later in their tearoom, eating lemon ice cream.

Fanny would never give her recipes. "Not even to the family?" I had asked. She explained that she could not give her experience, and what other people made with the recipe didn't taste like hers. So many people accused her of leaving out the "secret ingredient" that she stopped giving the recipes. "Most of them come out of the common cookbooks," she admitted, "but I can't give the experience in my fingers or nose or eyes." To prove her point, she took me to the kitchen and tried to teach me to make candy flowers. I worked, as long as my childish patience could bear, to make a lily like the one she made in less than a minute. Then I under-stood her wisdom.

At the train station I remembered my dad showing me a one-hundred-dollar bill, the first I had ever seen. I can't remember if he was returning from a trip or leaving on one.

An historical marker told me the city of Columbus was created in 1827 as a trading town on the Chattahoochee River near Coweta Falls. The site was selected because it was at the head of a navigable river and at the foot of a series of falls that offered potential water power. It had long been the site of a convergence of Indian routes. Twelve thousand acres were reserved for the town and commons. Surveying for streets and lots began in 1828. All lots were sold in a year. Within another year, the town had 1,000 inhabitants.

Grandmother's

George Parker Swift I, pioneer cotton manufacturer of Georgia, came from Massachusetts in the 1840s and started making cotton thread and yarn. He soon expanded into cotton weaving. In Columbus, he founded Muscogee Mills (now Muscogee Manufacturing Company), which has operated continuously since 1867. Its noon whistle still blows for Columbus at one of the largest manufacturers of cotton towels and ticking in the world. During the War between the States, the Eagle Mill, built in 1851, made cotton and woolen goods, including grey uniform tweed, cotton duck for tents, cotton stripes for army shirts, jeans, and other products. Federal forces burned that mill in 1865. It was rebuilt the next year, and its name changed to Eagle & Phoenix Mills to signify its rebirth.

The Columbus Iron Works made cannon and war munitions, and two gunboats. It later made ice machines. Haiman's Sword Factory was the largest plant of its type in the South, during the war. It was started in the 1830s as a tinsmith shop by two Prussians, and developed into the sword factory. Later, it also made cutlasses and Navy Colt pistols. (Guess who burned it in 1865!)

The oldest mill, on the river at Columbus, was at Coweta Falls. It ground corn meal. Known as Jones Mill, it was built in 1828. The original wooden dam across the river was replaced in 1906 and 1907 by a stone dam. Renamed City Mills, it ground meal for over a hundred years but closed for good in 1991.

I drove by the original RC Cola building. The water tank in the shape of a bottle is gone. Many people know that RC Cola originated in Columbus. Few are aware that Dr. John Styth Pemberton developed several medicines as a druggist in Columbus before moving to Atlanta in 1869. There, in 1886, he devised the formula for Coca-Cola. Two years later, he sold all of his interest in it for $1,750. I remember my grandmother grousing and groaning that she had made the mistake of selling her Coca-Cola stock. This made such an impression on me as a youngster that the first stock I ever bought was Coca-Cola. I only own a few shares, and I haven't sold it yet.

Most everyone knows "St. Elmo" as one of the most exquisite examples of restored, classic homes in America. I found it curious that it was actually called "El Dorado," when the popular author of *St. Elmo* and other Victorian novels lived in Columbus. The author, Augusta Jane Evans, was born in 1835, in "Wildwood." (For many years, water from springs there was channeled through hollow logs to supply the city of Columbus.) She spent the productive years of her literary career in Mobile, Alabama, but visits to her aunt at "El Dorado" inspired her celebrated novel, *St. Elmo.* In 1875, the name of the house was changed to the title of the novel.

Before this trip, I had thought it was only Oglethorpe's reputation that crossed the state, but apparently he traveled inland too. In 1739, having received word that the French and Spanish were exploiting Indian grievances against Carolina traders and encouraging war with the British, Oglethorpe came to a meeting of the Creek Nation at Coweta. The Chickasaws and Choctaws were also to send delegates to this Lower Creek town. Oglethorpe came with a few men from Fort Fredrica, made the Treaty of Coweta in 1739, then went to Augusta for further conferences with the Indians. He received promises of support from them, if England became embattled with her enemies. England did, gaining Florida from the Spanish, and eventually the Mississippi valley from the French.

Time for touring was running out. I went to see my Aunt Kathryn, now living at a retirement home. To get there I bumped slowly, several times, over the railroad tracks which had carried the Ringling Brothers Barnum and Bailey Circus to town. Until they had their own children, Aunt Kathryn and Uncle Frank took me every year to watch the circus unload from the trains. I always thought it was the best part of the whole show; better than cotton candy, peanuts, and sawdust in your shoes; better than the clowns and the high-wire acts — better to see the fire hose give a drink to a wide-mouthed hippopotamus and watch the elephants eat and work; better to watch the roustabouts carrying things everywhere. Perhaps it was the beginning of my fascination with what goes on backstage. Maybe that's why I liked working for the Central Intelligence Agency. From backstage you can see more; out front you only see the play.

My aunt and uncle never ceased to be the wonderful surrogate parents I remember. Sometimes I hear a familiar bit of wisdom, or the ring of their laughter, when I visit their children. On weekend visits to their cabin near Elbeck Mill, they taught me to love the country, to eat scuppernongs, and to watch, fascinated, as my uncle pursued his hobby of taxidermy. I always wanted to play in the box of bird eyes, but that wasn't allowed. My aunt was fine, and I was glad to talk over old times with her and catch up on stories of her children and family.

Sue and I reached the farm house about the same time, she from work and me from town. We'd both had a good day, and exchanged stories at supper.

Cataula, Sunday, April 7

Sue was spending the day with her mother, but we planned to meet late in the afternoon and plant a few more trees before supper. While it was good for the trees already planted, rain on the newly scraped road meant that we would have to walk across the creek again, and carry the trees. Sue didn't want to drive the truck over soft wet clay and get stuck, or make ruts that would be in the road all summer.

My day off from tree planting began with my pedaling north to visit Callaway and Pine Mountain. Who could come so near without visiting Callaway Gardens? I'd planned a whole day there during this trip, to quietly wander around and take photographs, especially in the Day Butterfly Center.

For the first few miles, my legs felt tired and sluggish. After I reached Hamilton — a few hills and five miles later — they felt better. Someone told me that all monuments to the Confederacy in Georgia faced the same direction: north. I hadn't noticed it myself, but the monument in the Hamilton square to Confederate soldiers of 1861-1865 had a fully uniformed soldier on top of a high column — facing north. Hamilton is an attractive town, ready for tourists, with dining, bed and breakfast, motel, and a marker to B. F. White, a song writer who lived from 1800 to 1879. He was mayor and a teacher in Hamilton, and published *Sacred Harp: A Singing,* a hymnal that saw well over a dozen editions.

Standing in front of the county seat courthouse for Harris County, I read that it was named in 1827 for Charles Harrison. An eminent Savannah jurist, he was born in England, educated in France, and served as Savannah's alderman or mayor for 20 years, refusing higher offices. Anyone who thinks Georgia was settled by a lot of uneducated, penniless stragglers wandering off a sailing ship couldn't be more inaccurate! On the contrary, the people who came to found Georgia towns and run the governments and economies, were educated, international citizens. Some say they were third sons of well-to-do English families, probably the same type of men I found in Southeast Asia during the 1950s, running rubber plantations and related businesses.

Another marker — it seems every courthouse square in Georgia has a minimum of three — told me the bell I was looking at was presented to Harris County by the LST 822 USS *Harris County,* in 1944. The bell was well traveled. It had been on the ship when she led 14 convoys through enemy waters without a casualty and participated in the invasion of Okinawa, the occupation of Japan, training at Inchon, and the retaking of Iwo Jima. The ship ferried supplies during the Korean War, and evacuated people from French Indochina. In June 1955, she went on a resupply mission to the Arctic.

Through town, US 27 is called Old College Street, for there was a college in Hamilton at one time. I followed it until I got to the shoulder of Pine Mountain, where the Callaway Country Store is located. There I learned that the wild muscadine grape and its relative, the scuppernong, were mentioned by William Bartram. He noted that the Indians gathered quantities of the wild grapes, some of which they dried for winter use. (Did the California raisins actually originate in Georgia?) I'd eaten many off the vine, and occasionally one can buy them in Georgia markets in season. The store sold jellies made from them.

I ate some popcorn and candy, then continued to pedal up the ridge road, GA 190, to the F. D. Roosevelt State Park Visitor Information Center. It was a spot Roosevelt used for picnics in the 1930s. I remembered when the stone house visitor's center was a hotel or inn, and didn't feel enough like pedaling back up to go down the mountain to the Little

White House, which I had seen during my last visit to Georgia. Up here on the mountain ridge, I recalled spending several painting sessions with my father while he did sketches. His best watercolor from this ridge is in Sarah and Francis McCullough's living room.

I also noted the Pine Mountain Trail, which Neal Wickham has devoted so much of his volunteer life to creating. I still hoped to visit his shop and meet him again — for the first time since grade school. Apparently, his sports store is a headquarters for Columbus outdoor enthusiasts.

Also along the ridge road, at one of the overlooks, I met three guys, a soldier from Fort Benning and his father and brother, visiting from California. The drought in California was so bad that the two visitors couldn't get over all the green vegetation, and wanted me to take a family picture with green background, using their camera. I did.

Then I rolled down to the Callaway Gardens entrance, planning to take photos of the azaleas and the butterflies, but the line of cars waiting to get inside was extremely long. From the mountain, I had seen the cars inside driving bumper to bumper. Not waiting proved to be a sound decision.

All the way back over Pine Mountain and down the other side, the clouds got darker. About six miles from the farm, I ran into a headwind, and it rained hard — quite hard for a few minutes. Then the weather blew on by and I began to dry out, though it was still quite dark and somewhat foggy. I got off the bike, turned on the caution light on the rear of my rack so that it blinked orange every second, then continued pedaling to the farm. When I got there, I cooked the chain and replaced it. Sue and I planted tomatoes instead of trees because more rain threatened, then came.

That night, after spending an hour on the telephone arranging the next two days, I read a book about a famous family and restaurant in Columbus. Written by Sara Spano, it was titled *I Would Have Written "Gone With the Wind" but My Cousin Margaret Beat Me to It*. It was as amusing as it sounds.

Cataula, Monday, April 8

On her way to town, Sue drove me to Lynnhaven, where the Audubon Society people do some of their work. Florence Lynn, whose home it is, met us at the door. She recognized me from photographs in the morning paper, and showed us the article Sandra Okamoto had written. Florence knows Sue's mother, Bet Blackmar, who has an extensive knowledge of plants and birds. Sue and Florence visited while I read the article. I was astounded that I could find no inaccuracy in it. I read it again with the same result. Furthermore it was interesting, certainly the best article that had ever been written about my bicycle adventures.

Florence has arranged to will her property to Columbus College. In the meantime, students and Audubon people work to keep it up as a bird sanctuary. The place is a treasure! Jane Knight, who had invited me there, arrived. In spite of drizzle, we walked all over. Jane explained the property arrangement, a wonderful solution for Florence, who is a delightful, cheery person in her seventies with no close relatives. Instead of having to leave her home, which is too much for her to maintain, friends come for frequent visits and help her. Recently, for example, Tom Breazeale made a bench of split cedar and placed it at a good location for watching the lake or the woods. Florence has a job feeding the birds and greeting her unfeathered guests.

During our walk, Jane and I found a luna moth wing. It looked like it belonged to the same creature that was under my picnic table at Trader's Hill Campground. Then she showed me a hophornbeam tree. Its strong wood was used for oxen yokes, mallets, wedges, cogs, or levers.

We had our binoculars, and Jane spotted a wood thrush. For some time, we watched it feeding under the bushes. It was the first one I had seen when I was sure I knew what I was looking at.

There were red buckeyes that had not been affected by the blight that killed the chestnut trees. The red buckeye flower is attractive to birds.

Along a brook, Jane pointed out lady fern, royal fern, and Christmas fern. As we proceeded, she identified black oak, pignut hickory, and yellow (tulip) poplar. Sue had told me the forester said not to cut the tulip poplar for it grows fast and would be a good lumber crop. Jane showed me a crane-fly orchid leaf with two colors of green on the top and purple underneath.

Many of the trees were growing their pollen on little worm-like things called catkins. We passed ebony spleenwort, spiderwort, and a trillium, also known as "little spotted Betsy."

The multitude of holes in a small beech tree were made by a sapsucker. We saw wild ginger and several wild azaleas. I've grown especially fond of azaleas because they are so hardy, even I can grow them in my garden at home. On these wild azaleas, small balls made of stockings filled with human hair, replaced from time to time, keep the deer from eating the plants. In bloom were the wild flame (orange) azalea and a tall pink variety.

While we were looking at an ancient red oak, we heard an owl that Jane said was a screech owl. What fun to be with such a knowledgeable guide! I had greatly enjoyed her small golden book, *Through My Watching Window.*

Later, we saw a red-shouldered hawk. Nothing moved on the lake, though we sat on the new bench and watched for a while. We hadn't seen many birds, but I was thrilled by the visit, and by Jane's company and help. She drove me to the Columbus Museum, where I met my cousin, Frank Schnell, museum archeologist.

Since my last visit a whole new building had been added to the museum, and it was magnificent! It is the second largest museum in the state. Citizens of Georgia owe it to themselves to visit. We went all over, talking furiously. I was particularly impressed by the children's play areas, and what could be learned and enjoyed there. What interested me most, though, was the Chattahoochee Legacy exhibit. Since it was Monday, the museum was closed, and there was no one to run the film. Frank's explanations were wonderful, and much of what he told me wasn't written on the exhibit cards. On return I would read and look more closely. It was too much for one visit anyway.

One of my favorite exhibits was the Prehistoric Indian Dwelling. Frank explained that its construction was all based on archeological data, as accurate as could be, except for the height of the sleeping benches. They knew they should be higher than a flea would jump, but no one on the staff knew how high fleas jumped in 1400 A.D., so they guessed. The dwelling reminded me of the living quarters of a nomad family in the mountains of Kashmir, which I visited one afternoon during a trek in the Himalayas.

Driving to lunch in his van, Frank revealed another new hobby he'd adopted since I last saw him. He had become an amateur radio operator, tag number KC4EXR. Like his father, Frank is a renaissance man who does everything well. In 30 seconds, he fixed an annoying problem in my computer software. Then he went on, recounting how members of MARS (Military Affiliate Radio System) had worked as volunteer radio phone operators, patching through calls to and from service personnel in Saudi Arabia. They would take incoming messages off the air and phone or mail them to the recipients.

For lunch, we went to Dinglewood Pharmacy, a fixture in Columbus, where I ate the famous scrambled dog — a hot dog with chili slathered all over it, onions on top, and oyster crackers on the side, washed down by sweet tea. Delicious!

Before he went back to work, Frank dropped me off at his house to visit with his wife Gail. Their son, Greg, was at school but I heard about his music projects. He was the only Georgian in a Sousa annual band concert in Washington, D.C. Gail and I had a splendid family visit before I pedaled back to the farm, via Moon and Hamilton roads. On the way, near the Cataula post office, I read on the historical marker that "Cataula" was Creek Indian for "Big Rock."

Sue had been working on taxes all day, and felt better for the progress she had made. I'd bought a number of *Columbus Ledger-Enquirer* papers and sent Sandra's article, with splendid photos by Mike Haskey, off to friends. Then I had to spend several hours on the phone, trying to understand and sort out problems created by the person who failed to help keep my house in order. Packages were not sent; bank deposits were not made. This presented Carol and Dorothy with additional problems to unravel. I was upset and didn't sleep well, which made me slow and groggy just when I wanted to be at my best the next day. It isn't easy to drop out of normal life for two months, even with lots of help.

Cataula, Tuesday, April 9

"People and their cultures have been closely tied to rivers throughout history," I read. "The Chattachoochee River has been the center of human activity for over 10,000 years. It has served as a food resource, a means of transportation and industry, a political boundary, and a line of communication. It made a Georgia poet famous, too. It has been both a unifying force and a refuge of diversity. The river has served not only as focal point of regional culture, but also as a pivotal influence of historical development beyond the region.

"This gallery, in the Columbus Museum, is dedicated to understanding of our region's role in cultural development and an understanding of the role of the individual within the stream of history. It is dedicated to promotion of an understanding of this diverse heritage through the audio visual impact of the motion picture and experience of the living space and the magic of the original object — the legacy of those who lived here before us."

I read the introduction while Frank arranged to have "The Chattahoochee Legacy" film rolled for us.

Nothing I had seen in Washington, at the National Geographic Society or the Smithsonian, was better. Not only was the quality of vision and sound exciting, but it was about my home.

Then I sped off to appear on "The Rozelle Show," a local talk show — an appearance that Jane Knight had arranged. I'd never done a studio television interview live. It was fun and interesting. I could watch the camera operators and the screen, to see what was transmitted, while the other two people were interviewed. Rozelle was a delightful, charming person and I felt honored to be included on her show.

As a result of Sandra's newspaper article, a local ABC affiliate, WTVM, wanted to interview me at the farm. Denise Schwab wanted to show my departure the next morning, so I explained what I planned to do, packed up my bicycle, and pushed it down the driveway for David Tonogan's camera, after Denise did the interview. Then we went along the road I would be taking to get wheel-turning, pedaling footage of me. David was from Jacksonville, Florida. He was part Indian and would soon participate in an old-fashioned Indian wedding in Alabama. Denise came from Buffalo, New York. We chatted about places we liked there, while waiting for the clouds to move so the light would be the same in all the shots. I gained enormous respect for the time and work that goes into producing the sports footage that I so enjoy when I'm a couch potato. I was really surprised when they told me I'd be on the 11:00 P.M. news that night.

It was a good thing to get so much media encouragement; otherwise, I might have just stayed on the farm and continued to rattle around Columbus and visit. Having proclaimed my intentions, so publicly and so often, kept me focused. On the one hand, I was eager to complete the tour I had laid out; but on the other hand, I wasn't looking forward to pedaling more lonely roads with my heavy load. For days, I had debated the pros and cons of giving tent, cooking equipment, and everything marginally essential to Sue, to take to my Possum Trot house. I really like to camp, though, and there were several fine state parks in north Georgia. Surely I would stay at two or three of them. If I didn't take the tent, that option was removed. So I went through everything, and slimmed my pack down quite a bit — faster than slimming myself! Tomorrow I would pedal north, leaving a long "next time" list of people and places to see in and around Columbus.

In mid-afternoon, when the Channel 9, WTVM crew left, Sue and I ate lunch, then jumped into her truck. We rattled over the Georgia red clay roads and through the woods, to the former turn-around, loading, and tree-topping sites. There we spent the rest of the afternoon dibbling holes (my job) and planting trees (Sue's job).

Black clouds rolled over us, while the wind rustled the surrounding trees. The black labrador, Lady, chased anything that moved, and occasionally found a deer or something to bark about. Songbirds kept up pleasant music, with a nearby pileated woodpecker providing timpani, while an occasional owl hoot punctuated quiet times. Four hours slid pleasantly by, and about 600 trees slid into the moist, soft earth. We joked, drank water, ate apples, and then tramped back to the truck before dark.

I fell asleep during Sue's telephone hour, but she woke me in time to watch myself pedal out of sight on the first mile from Cataula to West Point, ending the 11:00 p.m. news. They had done a good job on the story. Tomorrow, I would do it for real.

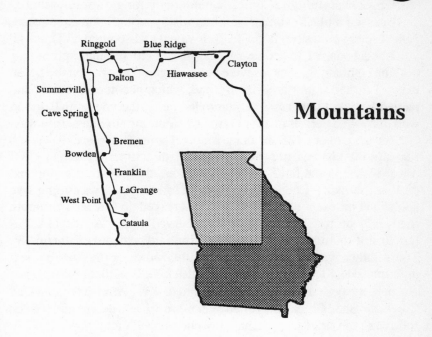

Mountains

Cataula, Wednesday, April 10

Sue prepared cheese grits, bacon, and juice for breakfast, and we lingered. I was mighty tempted to plant trees one more day and postpone the pedaling. But I had arranged to meet the Johnsons that night in LaGrange, so at mid-morning I got on my trusty Centurion and pedaled down Grant Road, headed for West Point and north Georgia. I'd left most of my clothes with Sue, and was wearing a 100% cotton T-shirt instead of the faster-drying, neon green shirt. This shirt was white, with a large red arrow and the words "Keep Left" printed on the back.

Grant Road took me to GA 315, where there was a closed W. B. Grant store with a rusty Coca-Cola sign. The bike didn't wobble or fishtail. It felt more like my old touring bicycle, except the tires were different. Why is it in America that every time we manufacture something really first class, of good quality, it is soon discontinued? It doesn't matter what field — bicycle tires, cooking utensils, nylon stockings, everything. Maybe I should lobby for anti-obsolescence.

I passed a black woman walking briskly along. She announced, "Oh! I seen you last night on TV." I waved and shouted a "Thanks."

I had been off the road a week, and could see that spring was moving right along. Leaves were beginning to come out on the pecan trees. I turned right on Fortsom Road, which becomes GA 315, and passed a white metal cross. It reminded me of the young girl, drunk, who had killed herself in a car crash at the entrance to Sue's driveway.

I crossed over I-185 and made a mental note of the best exit to reach Sue's farm. I had written, and misplaced, directions to reach GA 103 toward West Point, but I was enjoying the ride too much to stop and look at the map. I missed the short cut and knew I was going five additional miles, but I didn't care. I just stayed on GA 315, a smooth road with no traffic, as it gradually curved south. At the GA 219 junction, a customer in a food-gas station said he had seen me on TV. The weather was lovely as I pedaled the rollies north. At the next junction, I decided to keep straight on Lick Skillet Road, for it stayed closer to the perimeter of Georgia and led to West Point. I crossed Oak Creek and Sand Creek, and rolled over more ups and downs and creeks, following the ridge of the Chattahoochee River Valley.

A lot of the land was planted in trees, and I wondered how much longer that would be possible. Some people think trees aren't worth the investment any more. With a 15 to 30 year wait for them to grow, both land and investment are tied up. Then, when logging occurs, all the taxes have to be paid at once. Sue was planting for her children. Thousands of people are selling their land to developers, so they can invest in something else and get an annual income. No wonder our wetlands, hunting lands, and forests are being developed. Laws made to accomplish one purpose often detract from others.

After about 35 miles, I reached West Point and pedaled around a few blocks, looking for a place to eat lunch. I decided on Norman's Outdoors. It was almost 2:00 P.M. One table was occupied by three women. Along with the owner, Frank Norman, they watched while I took off helmet, gloves, and sunglasses, found some money, leaned the bicycle against the storefront, and walked in.

Frank said he was a bicyclist, too. He and his wife ride mountain bikes. He asked where I was going. Like so many others, he wistfully said, "I'd like to go with you," handing me my lunch. The three women asked me to join them. They were Maria Sagiuer, Joyce Bryan, and Lucy Champaian. They walk five miles daily, and were celebrating Lucy's 50th birthday. I sat down and began eating while they plied me with questions, saying they had wanted to get into bicycling but didn't know exactly where to begin. I suggested asking Frank, joining the local club, preparing themselves, and riding in the BRAG this year. We talked and ate as Frank prepared to close. His place had only been open two weeks. It was really attractive — part gift shop and part deli, right on 3rd Avenue, which seemed like a main street. Dave Shirley, a photographer, came in to get something, and they asked him to take our photo. I hope Lucy didn't feel we forgot her birthday. We talked about many things and had a grand time but she should have been the center of attention.

Out front, Frank joined us for more photos. They advised I should stay on 3rd Avenue and head straight up the west bank of the Chattahoochee River to the West Point Lake Dam, where there was a park. I could then pedal over the top of the dam, see the visitor's center, and come into the highway further north. It would be more scenic, and I wouldn't have to retrace my route. We all hated to part.

I pedaled north, still in Georgia, as they had suggested. It was a grand route I would not have known about without local help. Probably the road went into Alabama and came back without my realizing it.

A marker on County Line Road told me that an ancient town of the Muscogee Indians, called Ocfuskooche Tallahassee, meaning "Old Town," had stood there when English traders visited in 1685. The road was known as Old Horse Path. Settlers arrived about 1790, bitter fighting followed, and the town was abandoned. The inhabitants then moved west to the Tallapoosa River.

I stopped briefly at the Hardley Creek Park, at the foot of the dam on the west bank. It was a wonderful place. It had a fish pond for children under twelve that was being used by several families. I met a Cambodian mother and her child at a picnic table. I didn't understand her well, but gathered she had been in Georgia about ten years. She said the words "military camp," so I assumed she was the wife of a soldier.

As I pedaled up to the road that crossed the dam, the vast and beautiful West Point Lake came into view. There was not a cloud in the sky. The sun was warm. A glorious afternoon! Crossing the dam, I could hear, and feel, vibrations from the turbines below and the water coming out the bottom. I felt like I was rolling on top of a giant, humming electric clock.

A blue bird sitting on a "No Parking" sign didn't budge as I went by.

The visitor's center had displays about the Lower Creek Indians, traders, and settlers in the 1600s. British colonists from South Carolina traded goods, manufactured in Charles Town, for deer skins. Spanish missionaries tried to establish missions, but were expelled from the river valley. By the early 1800s, settlers began arriving in large numbers and soon drove the Creeks out of the region. West Point, however, remained a small outpost, while the settlers slowly cleared land and built cotton plantations. Water-powered industries followed, encouraging the trade routes. A number of floods — in 1886, 1900, and 1961 — slowed progress. The slide show ballyhooed the U.S. Army Corps of Engineers, and claimed that West Point Lake was developed as a demonstration area to promote nature, wildlife, and recreation. Who are they kidding? They built it for flood control and power generation to promote business!

I'd never been to LaGrange, and wanted to have time to look around before meeting the Johnsons and Doug Mote. US 29 was a good ride, and following the suggestions of my lunch companions I had no trouble turning off onto Old West Point Road, through farms, then back to US 29 just outside of LaGrange. Near the college, I asked a woman out walking if the street would lead me to the courthouse. She said it would. More interesting, though, was her response when I asked how she felt about all the BRAG bicyclists who came through last year.

"They were wonderful. I was surprised, too. There were tents completely covering the athletic fields," she motioned to them, "and around many of the campus buildings. When I went out for my walk in the morning, they were gone. It was amazing! There was not a scrap of paper, a styrofoam cup, a plastic bag, nothing. They were so clean, I wondered if I'd imagined them. We hope they will come back to LaGrange."

"Bicyclists are good folks," I agreed. "You should get to know them next time."

I stopped at a filling station and called Doug Mote's house again. I had called several times in the last day or so, to find out where he lived and to confirm that we would be using his telephone to coordinate our get-together. No answer — again. He had said Gail might be out of town. I hoped he wasn't gone, too. How would I ever find the

Johnsons? First, I had to find Doug's house. The woman walking hadn't heard of his street, nor had the woman at the next telephone. She said her husband worked at the police station and suggested I ask there, giving me directions to it. (I'd thought of the fire department; they have to have good maps, and knowledge of their area.)

At the square, I stopped to look around. I asked a policeman standing on the corner if he knew where Phillip Green Road was. He had never heard of it, either, but he pulled out his radio and asked headquarters. They didn't know where it was, but said they would check further. The policeman had been a Marine for many years and had an engaging smile. The station called him back, and he laughed. We both felt better when he told me what they said. "The name of that road was recently changed. It is now Old West Point Road." He began to explain how to get there, but I interrupted, "I just came that way, so now I'll go back."

I went so far back, I was beginning to mumble about the Moteses living in West Point instead of LaGrange. Then, I saw some people in their yard and waved. Out of water, and running out of patience, I put down my bike and walked to their house. As they filled my water bottle, I asked if they knew the house number I was looking for, several hundred digits from their number. I also wanted to be sure this really was the former Philip Green Road. They laughed, confirmed the name, and said a lot of people have that trouble. They knew the Moteses well, and told me how to find their house. It wasn't far — less than a mile.

When I reached the Moteses' house, no one was home, and I could hear the phone ringing inside. That would be the Johnsons, trying to find me. I sat down to wait and drank some water, glad at least that I didn't have to pedal anymore, or backtrack any further, after 62 miles. Ten minutes later, the phone rang again. I checked the whole house thoroughly. The doors were all locked, and no windows were open, except a high one where the cat sat, looking out. "Well, I'll wait a while before breaking in, and hope the Johnsons continue to call." They did, every ten minutes. To alleviate my frustration, I plugged my computer into an outlet I had found in the carport and typed notes from my dictation tapes.

Finally, I decided that if Doug didn't come back by 8:00 P.M., I would go next door and ask to use the telephone. I didn't know where the Johnsons were staying, but setting a deadline for doing something helped. Every time the phone rang — for over an hour — I paced. At 8:00 P.M., I headed next door and met an elderly woman who said she didn't know the Moteses well."Are they the people with bicycles on their car roofs?"

"Yes."

"Well, he drove off with his bicycle a while ago, about three hours ago."

She agreed I could return and use her phone, if needed. I was stepping out the door when Doug turned into the driveway. He'd been to West Point, riding with his buddies, on a route over the dam. He must have left just after I passed his house the first time, or he would have seen me on the road. He unlocked the door and the phone rang!

We did all get together for supper, and we had good laughs with Earl and Diane Johnson, recapping our frustrations. We didn't get into our beds until midnight — but I would have company on the road tomorrow. Earl and Doug were going to ride with me.

La Grange, Thursday, April 11

Doug and I drove to the other side of LaGrange to pick up Earl for breakfast, leaving our bicycles at Doug's house. We put my panniers in Diane's car and agreed to meet at the Horne's house in Bremen, after she finished working. We took Earl's bicycle back with us. Our logistics got complicated; we did it so that I could ride with an unencumbered bicycle. Both the men had racing wheels and were stronger riders. Reducing my load minimized these differences. I was dragging a bit from lack of sleep, and probably from the tension of last night's missed communications. Naturally, I compounded this fatigue by following too much supper with too much breakfast.

Back at the Moteses' home, Doug showed Earl and me how he and Gail store their bikes and wheels on a rack he built into the spare bedroom. They have fine bikes and a great many bicycle paintings, awards, and sculptures. Doug said his bike computer also showed 23.9 for the time trial route near Columbus. He had compared mileage with several other riders, after riding the expected 24.2 course, and they had agreed. My bike computer was okay.

Doug's bike club, Fairdinkum, has no dues, officers, or rules. It's just a group who like to ride and share training and help each other. At the time trial, they were all wearing their Fairdinkum jerseys. I liked the red, green, and white stripes; they were visible and attractive, and I liked the message. They thought of calling the club Border Patrol or Dam Bicycle Club, but selected Fairdinkum from an advertisement about Australia. Anything fairdinkum is excellent — fairdinkum blokes, fairdinkum Aussies, fairdinkum statements. Eventually, they expect to get more formal, and join the Southwestern Velo Club in Columbus with whom they often ride.

Earl said he gets lost all the time, so he never rides alone. He would be glad to go wherever I wanted to go. He is slim and strong and charges up hills at about the same pace he goes on the flats, which is what you are supposed to do. He said if he got ahead not to worry, he would wait.

We left Doug's house, and he guided us north, via Whitaker and Cameron Hill Road, to GA 219 and 34 (complete with a road repair detour), into Franklin. As soon as we came to a hill, Earl went ahead. Doug had suffered a bad fall and injury a year ago, and wasn't back to racing form. He said riding to Franklin and back was a long ride for him, almost triple his usual training ride. But I'm sure the pace was slower.

Doug is an entertaining raconteur, and since the roads were free of traffic, he rode beside me, recounting tales of his first bicycle at age five, and his many races at state and national levels. Doug had pedaled all over as a boy. When he finally got a mileage indicator for his bicycle, it surprised him that the first day it registered 67 miles. He had begun winning all the local races, and eventually went to a bigger race, with experienced bicyclists. Imitating their cycling pants, he cut off some old black jeans, put on his brightest T-shirt, and wore an old hockey helmet he had found in the barn. He went to the race, expecting to show those big-city fellows how to do bicycling, but instead learned how to learn. Doug finished second or third from last out of about a hundred, and came home committed to winning next time. He joined a club, trained, learned, and won. Doug's experience was a good example of the notion that every success is the result of many failures.

I would adore having Doug for a coach. But I live too far away. I need to learn good riding and handling technique though I don't expect to race. As in tennis, or any other sport, you can learn only so much on your own. Eventually, you need to pedal with the pros. I've had a lot of help all along, especially technical advice from Floyd Hartman. He could help me with training, too, if I stayed home long enough to let him.

While I was on this trip, seven people in the Washington, D.C., area were training for the Paris-Brest-Paris race, which is held every four years. August of 1991 was special, because it was the centennial. Entry requires two years of qualifying races. Training bikers usually do long-distance rides, 100 to 200 miles, on Saturdays, and a 50-mile ride for fun, with friends, on Sundays. I rode the social 50-mile rides led by Crista Borras, stopping midway for lunch. Often the weather was bordering on winter, and I would not have gone 50 miles, or even five, alone. Thus had these friendly long-distance racers helped me train for my Georgia tour. I missed their company.

Doug admitted that he had waffled this morning about riding all the way to Franklin with us, not just because of the distance. Since his accident, he has been afraid to ride alone, something he grew up doing for hours at a time. Fear is a terrible dragon. I was proud that his desire to join us got him on the road, and was sure that returning to LaGrange alone after lunch would help calm this fear. Fear seems to expand the more you give in to and contract as you resist its effects.

In Franklin, we ate lunch at the Village Inn. Though Earl was often far ahead, he waited at all possible turns, so we actually kept together on the road rather well. A black puppy followed us for so many miles, we began to worry about it. At one point, we had to wait where some repaving was going on. We found a paper cup and filled it with water; the dog drank it all. It was beginning to limp, and after drinking the water, it lay down and didn't follow when we continued.

Everyone in Franklin seemed to eat at the Village Inn. There were old women, young families, highway workers, farmers, the head of the county highway department, the road crews, chief of the department of transportation, and an old man who stopped in for dessert and coffee. It was busy, friendly, small, and comfortable. Tables filled as soon as people left, but there was no line. The food was excellent and I finally ate sensibly, catching up on vegetables, greens, yams, pinto beans, corn bread, and sweet tea, but I couldn't resist the lemon meringue pie.

We talked about how nice the "silk sheets" road had been, and about problems of bicycle clubs. Doug explained that the Columbus clubs had been reorganized several times. They have difficulty dealing with the varied goals and abilities of members. There are so many styles and types of riding and so many types of bicycles: racing, mountain, recreation, city, track, and hybrid bicycles, kids' bicycles, beach bikes, and tandems, each with a different type and style of rider. In addition, riders on any bicycles vary widely in ability and goals. There are long- and short-distance tourists, racers of many kinds, casual, recreational, and mountain riders. Earl declared that every club in Georgia has the same problems, but they are solvable. I maintained that every club in the country has those problems, and they are indeed solvable. Beginners need mentors and racers need an audience.

After lunch, we recrossed the Chattahoochee River. I knew that I was seeing it for the last time on this tour. At the top of the hill junction, Earl and I would continue north. I tried to encourage Doug by telling him he wouldn't be alone, the puppy was waiting for him. I had really enjoyed Doug's company, and was sorry that he had to return home.

Earl and I rolled north on GA 100 and, as I had hoped, it continued to follow a ridge toward Bowdon. The overcast sky made the light flat and gray. Our road was smooth. We passed an antique shop called Martha's Junksion and cattle farms with fertilized pasture of lush, green grass. Sue had taught me to recognize quality pasture. When I caught up to Earl in Ephesus, he was stopped under a tree, changing his shirt. It was warmer. I yelled that my legs were just getting warmed up and kept going, knowing he would catch me quickly.

Entering Carroll County, we saw a lot of chicken houses. Then we passed a Baptist church built of random field stones. It was a beautiful building on a hill. I went soaring down the other side of the hill, into the outskirts of Bowdon, established in 1853 — population 1,853. I thought I'd ask directions at the fire house or a store, but a UPS truck turned into a garage, I motioned to Earl, and we followed it. I asked the driver how to get to Bremen on back roads, avoiding Tallapoosa and the major highways. He told me, and I marked my map. Meanwhile, Earl had asked the shop owner, Billy Crocker, who drew a map for us. We took a few photos and pedaled off.

Billy Crocker's mileages were exactly right. We made all the turns through Mt. Zion and Bowdon Junction, and came out on the north side of Callaway Airfield, as Doug had said we could.

From the McDonald's at I-20 and US 27, I called Karen Horne, who gave us directions that we followed to her house. We hadn't been there long when Diane Johnson drove into the driveway. Karen invited us all to stay for spaghetti supper, which we did. We had a fine time meeting her sons Andy and Matt, laughing, and telling stories of the road.

I had met Karen three years before on BRAG. Her tent happened to be next to mine and we were both alone, so conversation was natural. I was impressed by her because she was the only one in her family who bicycled, and she wanted to go on BRAG. Her husband and three sons had brought her to the start, set the tent up, and gone home. They would pick her up in Savannah. Karen had never done anything like BRAG before, and never even camped without her family. I admired her spunk and enjoyed her company during the rides. We usually put our tents close together at the end of the day. This was the first time we had seen each other since, and I was grateful for her support of my tour. Meanwhile, with her sons, she had been on the BRAGs I'd missed.

After supper the Johnsons went to a motel. Andy gave me his room when I told him that I'd get seasick trying to sleep on Matt's waterbed! Earl wanted to ride at least half the next day, and Diane would carry my stuff. Karen would join us, but the boys had to attend school. It looked like we had another grand day ahead.

Bremen, Friday, April 12

I heard the clock chime six times. I
lay in bed, listening to the car tires on the
road, trying to decide whether or not it
was still raining. The tires were making
more noise than they would on a dry road,
but less than in a steady rain, and occasionally a wheel splashed through a
puddle. It was getting dry. I looked out
the window for visual confirmation. There
was a trace of drizzle. When I opened the
window and sniffed, the air smelled of
earth and spring. It looked colder than it
was.

I went into the kitchen, where Karen
was preparing breakfast. She had invited
Earl and Diane to join us. On the counter
sat the largest mixing bowl of batter I'd
ever seen.

"What is that going to be?"

"Waffles."

"From scratch?"

"They are easy, and it is the only way to make them crisp."

"What makes them crisp?"

"Real egg whites."

"What do you do with the rest of the egg?"

"It goes in too, but the waffles are more crisp if the whites are
beaten stiff and folded in after the rest of the batter has been mixed.
Commercial places use liquid batter made of dried eggs. It just can't
get as crisp."

I could hardly wait. In cafes, I ask that my waffles be cooked
longer to make them crisp, but they just brown. When Karen served
our waffles, I ate the first one without anything on it because it was so
light and crunchy. The taste and consistency were marvelous!

The boys went to school, not quite unwillingly, for the mist
continued and the morning was gray, more conducive to reading a book
than pedaling a bicycle. Reluctantly, we agreed it just wasn't a good

day for travel. So we served ourselves more waffles, which Karen magically produced from the kitchen while eating with us. Her husband, Ed, had come in late and joined us for our second breakfast.

Rain pounded the house, accompanied by thunder and lightning. It turned much colder while we were eating. We sat around in our bicycle clothes, ate waffle after waffle, and talked. I'd not had a real "from scratch" waffle for so long. Karen kept saying they were easy to make. We kept eating and talking. The more we ate, the less we felt like pedaling, and the later it got. Finally, about 10:00 A.M., we decided the rain wasn't going to stop, it wasn't going to get warmer, and the weather forecast for tomorrow sounded better. We canceled pedaling and hoped for a dry Saturday.

Unfortunately, Earl and Diane had to get home. Earl was flying to Philadelphia that evening, to attend his son's wedding. Disappointed, we said our goodbyes. Karen repeatedly assured me I was welcome to stay at her home another night.

After Earl and Diane departed, Karen told me she had to go to Atlanta on business. She and Ed run their own business, which is hard enough, but at present they were running it from home, which seems to me to call for maximum self-discipline. I thought about typing notes about the trip or reading a book, but instead asked if I could ride along and keep her company. It would be a real rest day, having nothing to do with bicycling, compiling notes, or figuring out where to go next on which road. We spent a pleasant day chatting and driving, and between errands ate lunch at the OK Cafe. We returned in time for supper. It rained off and on all day. I was happy to do something dry. However, I would leave the next morning, no matter what!

Bremen, The Horne's House, Saturday, April 13

The early morning outlook wasn't much better than the day before, except that the mist wasn't so heavy and the road was almost dry. I was pleased that Karen wanted to ride with me despite the weather, and surprised that Andy, the younger boy, insisted on going. Matt wanted to come too, but he had promised to participate in a project. So, at a slower pace than a sunny morning would have evoked, we packed the bicycles, put on our helmets and gloves, waved goodbye to Ed and Matt, and pedaled north on US 27. Drizzle continued intermittently for a while. The road was damp, but the air was warm, and we were happy as soon as our wheels began to turn along the open road.

I rode behind Karen and Andy, telling myself I didn't want to set an uncomfortable pace for them. (The real reason was that I was feeling tired and lazy.) I passed a sign, "Chicken Litter $150," stuck in a pile in the back of a pickup truck. I'd never heard the term, and wondered whether it was like kitty litter. Were they selling it "clean" to the chicken farmers or "used" to the gardeners?

Before we knew it, we were in Buchanan, admiring the courthouse. Then we continued north, making good time. There wasn't much traffic on the road. We had begun our tour at 9:00 A.M. when early workers were at work and shoppers were probably still drinking coffee. We hollered back and forth, and occasionally rode two abreast when no cars were coming, but mostly we charged over the rolling hills.

Waffles had been just as good the second day, and had fortified us so well we hardly glanced at the grocery stores or cafes until we reached Cedartown. When I saw a barbecue sign and smelled the food, I felt hungry. Being in the lead at the time, I turned in. We got off the bikes, and I suggested that though it was too early for lunch, maybe we should have a snack — like half a barbecue each. It was delicious!

We went outside, put on our damp jackets, gloves, and helmets, and started to get on our bikes. Andy noticed he had a flat tire. There was a picnic table, so we leaned all the bikes against it and I sat down.

"Well, we'll just have to fix it. Only take five or ten minutes."

Apparently, neither of them had ever actually changed or patched a tube, so we had a lesson. I tried not to get my hands dirty, but eventually, we needed six hands to get the wet tire loose and the damp tube out to be replaced. Then we had to get it all back together. Finally, we washed our hands with water from our bottles and dried them on paper towels from the restaurant. Struggle and discussion and cooperation got us back on the road in half an hour. We hadn't intended to present a show for the people eating their barbecue, but that's how it turned out.

The rain had stopped. I was hungry again before we left, but I knew Cave Spring had a restaurant, so we proceeded northwest on GA 100, following a ridge through fields. It made a wonderful ride with even less traffic. We galloped along like young colts. We talked about BRAG encounters and places, and looked forward to the next BRAG in June.

Twenty-five miles from our start in Bremen, we passed a sign indicating Cave Spring, eight miles ahead, Coosa, 20 miles, and our destination, Summerville, 38 miles. The road was dry, and the sky continued to brighten. Karen saw eight turtles jump in the water as we passed; I heard the splash as she shouted to point them out. It was already past noon when I realized that for yet another day I had forgotten to set my Avocet at noon, which would make the bicycle stopwatch operate as a timepiece.

On a long, gradual assent, Karen asked me, with a glint of humor in her voice, "How do you like these famous, Georgia flat hills?" She meant they look flat. We were proceeding so slowly, and with such effort, that when we eventually looked back, we discovered we were climbing. From the bicycle seat, there often seems to be an optical illusion that makes you think you're going down when you are really pedaling up, or vice versa. For the rest of the day, we joked about discovering another "flat hill."

We passed the entrance to the Georgia School for the Deaf, entered the city limits of Cave Spring, and turned off our route into town.

After an excellent lunch at Shumate's Diner, we pedaled around the town, and looked at the cave entrance where the spring originated. I took some photos of the Montgomery Farm log cabin, which had been moved from Vann Valley to Rolater Park. We were dmiring the watercress, flourishing in the spring water that flows to the swimming pool, when Loretta Lindsey stopped to talk with us. She works at city hall, at the cave, and all year at the pool. She said the spring cave was being cleaned and repaired and would open soon, but the pool wouldn't open until summer. She recommended we see the original deaf school building, now city hall, and the other school buildings past the pool.

The marker at city hall informed us that in 1833, a deaf man, John Jacobus Flournoy of Jackson County, promoted education for the deaf. He interested Governor Wilson Lumpkin and the Georgia legislature in working toward this goal. At first the pupils, few in number, were sent to the American Asylum for the Deaf and Dumb in Hartford, Connecticut. But by 1846, with four deaf pupils in a log cabin, Flournoy had begun the school in Cave Spring.

On the lawn near the marker was a giant trampoline. Andy was already jumping on it and it looked such fun. Ever since I first saw one, and especially during the past five or six years, I have wanted to know how it feels to jump on a trampoline. This hankering probably originated at the circus, watching aerialists tumble down into the nets and bounce/walk on them. I climbed up and began to jump — gently. It was fun. Andy said if I landed on my seat, I'd pop right back up to my feet. I didn't. I scraped my elbows on the web, bounced a few more times, and climbed down. My great trampoline fantasy had been satisfied.

We felt comfortable in Cave Spring. It was historical, small, interesting, lovely — perfect for bicyclists. There were many roads in and out. The bed and breakfast in the park looked inviting, there were several places to eat, antique shops, the spring cave itself, and a soft atmosphere. I thought it would be a fine place from which to organize a weekend of bicycle rides.

Long before our interest was thoroughly satisfied, we pedaled past more renovated houses, out of town, and back to GA 100 north, continuing through Floyd County, until Foster's Mill Store and Bait Shop brought us to a halt. The signs were rusty, the wood was old, the whole building listed to the east, and close inspection revealed heart pine shutters on the windows. I opened the screen door and entered. The door slammed shut with authentic bang and clatter. Owner Joe Terry told us, from behind the counter, that we were in the oldest country store in Floyd County. Way back when, it had been the county courthouse. We bought drinks and snacks while prowling like a trio of cats, inspecting the potbelly stove, looking into the bait pool, taking pictures.

Customers asked us questions about our tour. One lady asked me where we had come from, and I replied, "Cave Spring, via GA 100."

"GA 100 doesn't go through Cave Spring."

"Yes, but that is how we came."

"GA 100 doesn't go to Cave Spring."

"We came on 100, turned off and went into Cave Spring then came here on 100."

"GA 100 doesn't go to Cave Spring."

"You're accurate, that is true, but we came from Cave Spring and we traveled most of the way on 100."

"You couldn't."

"Sorry, lady, you asked what we did, and I told you."

She left the store. I looked around at the other smiles, for I had been laughing. But I didn't like her telling me where I had been. Normally,

I would have been a bit more polite, but something in her tone of voice got my hackles up. Angry, I was tempted to pedal back and look at the signs, because I thought, in fact, that part of Route GA 100 joined Route GA 411 inside the city limits of Cave Spring. Instead, I ate some more popcorn and thought about something else.

We continued. The sun came out in the afternoon, warming the air. As we passed a house with a basket of white flowers hanging on the front porch, Karen called my attention to it, saying it indicated that someone in the immediate family had recently died. We pedaled along one valley that had ridges on both sides. Occasionally, we passed a sourwood tree in bloom. I'd been told that sourwood blossoms made the best honey. When the trip was over, I bought sourwood honey and agreed that it was excellent.

I was just wondering about the extraordinary number and size of high power lines when I crested a hill and saw a power station near Coosa. At the junction there was a sign about Dr. Elizur and Esther Butler, missionaries to the Cherokees, who were buried in graves nearby. Born in Connecticut and married in 1820, they were sent to the mission near Rome, Georgia, in 1826. Mrs. Butler died after eight years of service to the Cherokees. Two years later, Dr. Butler was arrested for residing in the Cherokee Nation without taking an oath of allegiance to the state of Georgia, and for failing to obtain a license from the governor. He was sentenced to four years of hard labor in the state penitentiary but was pardoned by Governor Wilson Lumpkin in 1833, almost a year after the U.S. Supreme Court nullified the law under which he was arrested. Upon release, Dr. Butler returned to the mission, but was forced to move the following year with the Cherokees, and continued to serve them until his death in Arkansas in 1857. Whether I agree with his message or not, he reaps high marks for commitment to his convictions.

We stopped at a store in Holland. Karen called Ed to tell him where to meet us in Summerville, nine miles ahead. I bought a bag of Smartfood popcorn, which we quickly devoured. We were all getting tired, and I was getting nervous about being on the road so late on Saturday afternoon. I had already seen one drunk fellow at the store. It was about 5:00 P.M., the day hadn't been sunny, and the clouds were closing in on us. The road appeared to be flatter, but we had a headwind into Summerville, so the rest of the ride was tough. We really were tired, but having Karen's and Andy's company had made the day special.

Going up a hill, Andy had trouble shifting gears and got into a higher rather than lower gear, which made pedaling impossible. I hadn't realized that he didn't understand what the gear levers were doing. He wanted to know if he pushed the lever forward, whether he would get a higher or lower gear. I told him I couldn't remember; I had to look when I changed, sometimes.

"What do I look at?"

"Good question."

So in the middle of the hill, we got off the bikes. Karen held up Andy's rear wheel; he turned the pedals and moved the levers to watch what happened. Gears are not really a mystery, if you understand what's going on.

"Andy, put the chain on the smaller wheel in front," I requested. "The big wheel in front is the highest gear. It has more teeth. You usually don't need it except going downhill. The rear cluster, called a freewheel, contains five to seven, or more, rings. The smaller ring, with the fewest teeth, is high gear, just the opposite of the chain wheels in front."

Andy rotated his pedals and got the chain on the lowest rear gear, with the most teeth. Now we were ready to start up the hill again. Karen said that she had never had these principles explained. So she rotated her gears to the lowest.

"Now, don't move the front of the chain, just move the back," I cautioned.

"Normally, when you begin a ride, look to be sure that the chain is riding on either the small or the middle chain wheel, and in the middle of the freewheel cluster. Then you can begin riding comfortably on a flat, smooth area. To make uphill pedaling easier, put the chain to a larger ring of the freewheel. When you go down, use a smaller ring. Eventually, you will do this automatically by the feel of the pedals, like shifting gears in a car by the feel of the engine.

"Once you get comfortable, and clearly understand the feel of the gear changes on the freewheel, then to gain more speed when going downhill, you can move to the large chain wheel in front. Use the "granny," or smaller chain wheel, for climbing, if your bicycle has one. It's easy to look down at the chain ring, to see where the chain is located, if it doesn't feel right. With a little practice, you can look back between your legs and see where the chain is riding on the freewheel. Look before and after each change, until you learn the feel. Be careful, however, because at first, when you look away from where you are going, the bicycle tends to wobble. That can be confusing to a vehicle driver behind you, and dangerous to you. Join a club, or ride with others who are willing to teach you, or read books and magazines that explain riding techniques."

I wondered how they had managed to ride so far — so fast — so frequently — in the wrong gear! Andy was a strong young boy, but not using the gears, or using them incorrectly, would strain even his young knees. I thought it best to add one more note of advice:

"Toward the end of a long ride, or at any time when you feel or become aware of your knees, it is best to ride in one gear lower, and spin your feet faster to maintain speed. This is called spinning, and saves your knees. You will not be a fast rider this way, but you will save your knees, and be able to continue when people pushing high gears are collapsed by fatigue or pained knees."

Our day on the pedals ended in Summerville, shortly before 6:00 P.M. GA 100 had been a wonderful, silk sheets, ridge or valley road all day. After 65 miles, we were more happy to have completed our ride than proud of what we had done. Pride in accomplishment would come tomorrow.

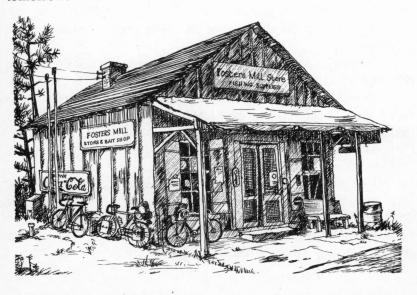

Andy and Karen decided to wait at the Waffle House for Ed to come pick them up. It was too cold, 65 degrees, and I was too tired, to stay in the Floyd State Park as I'd intended. I needed to find a motel before it got dark, and scouted around town, finally asking a sheriff in a police cruiser. There were two motels, on opposite sides of town, both run down. He suggested I would be all right in the Sequoyah — a few miles north. The motel was named for George Guess or Gist, the Sequoyah inventor of the Cherokee alphabet.

I brought this news back to the Waffle House, and decided I'd better get to the motel and check in. When Ed came, the Hornes would drive to the motel, or I would return to the Waffle House for dinner. I was sufficiently tired that once I stopped, it would be extremely difficult to get my legs to pedal again, so I was anxious to secure a room before I sat down to dinner.

It seemed extraordinarily far out US 27, a very long two miles. Just before I reached the motel, an opossum waddled across the four-lane highway right in front of me, stepped over the curb and sidewalk, and walked nonchalantly into the grass and undergrowth. I had never seen a live opossum, though it is common to see them dead on the road. It was a comical diversion from my fatigue. The animal waddled slowly, fur covering its round body, pointed nose and small eyes looking about, and raw-skin tail bringing up the rear. It proceeded with obvious unconcern and lack of fear. I'd read that the reason they get killed so often is that they freeze when they see lights, or walk toward them. Its rear feet seemed a bit pigeon toed, apparently the root cause of the waddle-walk.

Once in the motel room, I looked around carefully. The two light bulbs in the lamp worked, as well as the bathroom and bedroom ceiling lights; the window would open and the screen almost fit; the smell was tolerable, and I would use only the bottom sheet and my sleeping bag anyway.

I'd been out of water for some time, and decided to rehydrate before returning to town to meet the Hornes. Actually, I hoped that if I waited long enough, they would come in the car, and I wouldn't have to ride any further. After drinking two or three glasses of water, and lying on the bed to watch a little golf on TV, I got up, removed the panniers from the bike, and headed back toward town.

I'd only gone a mile when a car blinked its lights and turned into a driveway. Ed, Matt, Andy, Karen, and a friend of the boys tumbled out. They had decided to stop on the way home at a favorite Chinese restaurant, instead of eating locally. That suited me, for I was really too tired to eat. I was worried about Karen and Andy; the distance, combined with rolling hills, had really challenged them. It had challenged me too, and I'd been riding daily. After a round of hugs and good wishes and shouts of, "See you at BRAG," they piled into the car and turned south. I was sorry to see them go. It had been a splendid day. I was alone again. It is fine when I am accustomed to it, but at first, after good company has departed, it is hard. I looked across the street and saw a store. Mentally, I thanked the Hornes for coming to meet me, and cheered up inwardly knowing that I didn't have to ride further, and that a store was at hand. I bought food for the road tomorrow, and to eat in my room, and returned to the TV golf coverage. I drank and drank and drank water. Excessive thirst indicated how fatigued I was. It also confirmed that while I enjoyed all the marvelous company, I expend extra energy when people are around all the time. Physical, emotional, and mental energies were spent, and I'd been digging into reserves.

Tomorrow, I would proceed far enough to turn east. I knew that my iron horse Centurion, piloted by my now weakened will, would probably "smell the barn," and see no sights worthy of deflection. Home was calling, and the overcast days and cold rainy nights, often with thunderstorms, were urging me on.

I was no longer carrying the heavy sweatsuit, jacket, and hat that would have allowed me to sleep comfortably outside in such weather. Perhaps I could find more routes through valleys or along ridges, though somehow I had to pedal over several gaps, around Brasstown Bald, the highest mountain in Georgia, and into the Blue Ridge Mountains to reach my waiting house.

Summerville, Sequoyah Motel, Sunday, April 14

When I woke up I felt much better. I drank almost half a gallon of grapefruit juice. The rest I put in a water bottle on my bicycle, and, as usual, topped it up with water. I generally cut juices up to 50 percent with water, to get more liquid in my system. I was totally out of KM (a potassium supplement with herbs) and realized that without its help, I felt more tired than on my longest ride of over a hundred miles, from Louisville to Pooler. It seemed important to notice how tired I felt with and without the KM. For me, those 14 herbs and minerals make a great difference in my energy level and seem to flatten hunger cravings so I have less tendency to overeat. I take no vitamins, but consume large quantities of fresh fruit, juice, and vegetables, while limiting meat to chicken and fish. I also omit excess fat, salt, sugar, alcohol, and caffeine from my diet, and I eat smaller quantities more often, which, given the need of increased blood flow to support exercise, aids digestion. If I feel too sluggish, I'm careful not to mix protein and carbohydrates at the same meal, or within a couple of hours of each other, to eat fruits early in the day and other items later. I drink V8 when I don't get enough vegetables.

By 9:00 A.M. I was ready to go. I chuckled at my room number as I left; it had been a good night on the 13th of April, in Room 13. The sky was overcast, the road was dry, and there was neither mist nor rain. I began to pedal back to Summerville, then took GA 48 to Menlo, eight miles along the Julliette Gordon Low Highway.

I stopped to phone Mom, then Dottie, who was at my house in Washington. I found out that the tenant in my apartment had deposited no rent in my account since my departure. I wondered what the problem was, and why he always had some excuse for not paying until I returned from a trip, especially when I was counting on the rent. My rental house was empty and in the process of being repainted, so I'd made large outlays and had no income. Fury over the situation kept me turning the pedals up steep climbs to and through Menlo, and on up the mountain to Cloudland, where I turned onto the Lookout Mountain Highway along a ridge similar to the Blue Ridge Parkway.

At first it was a rather rough-textured surface, halfway between shake-and-bake and silk-sheets. "Shake-and-bake" is another term from BRAG. Many of the smaller county roads, though paved, are quite rough — Shake. The ride is held in June, when it is hot — Bake. I soon passed the entrance to Camp Julliette Low in Cloudland, Georgia. Later, I learned it had never been a Girl Scout camp, although there are many in the area, and is still a private camp.

As I continued rolling along the ridge, the clouds were so low I could see very little beyond the road. Moisture from the clouds had collected in spider webs, and they hung everywhere, like inverted parachutes. Blue and white wildflowers were in bloom. The blue flowers looked like huge violets. Dogwood and sourwood, wild cherry and black locust trees were blooming. Shortly before entering Walker County, I descended into an alpine meadow where I could see further under the overcast than in the clouds.

At a country store, 22 miles into the ride, I got off my bike stiff, cold, and hungry. I drank V8 juice, and coffee for internal heat, and ate some Smartfood popcorn from my bag. Warmed and rested, I asked the man running the store about route choices ahead. I expected to spend the night at Cloudland Canyon State Park. He said it was part-way up the mountain to Trenton, and that at the junction of 136 and 157 I would have three choices: left, straight, or right. Left would be up the mountain back into the clouds, where I would see nothing and be cold; straight, along this valley or ridge, would not take me anywhere for the night; and right, down the mountain to Cooper Heights, would take me across the state further south of the perimeter, through Dahlonega and Helen, to Rabun County.

None of the options sounded right. I wanted to see New Echota, the Cherokee capital, of special importance to Georgia history, but on that route I would wind up, after pedaling all day, only 18 miles north of where I spent last night! I wasn't sure I could cope, mentally, with riding up all these mountains all day, in this weather, to arrive almost where I started.

I left the store and continued through the valley, a pleasant ride into and out of Dade County, so that technically I had ridden through some portion of every county on the Georgia border so far. About 15 miles beyond that cup of coffee, I reached the junction of 157 and 136. It was decision time. I couldn't see anything beyond a hundred yards, and I was getting cold again. The only choice seemed to be to the right, east. Both other routes led deeper into the mountains — uphill and to camping. East led down to people and home.

I turned right, and within a hundred yards or so I was plunging down, at an ever-accelerating pace. At each curve I anticipated a horrid climb, yet continued to descend. I was cold before the downgrade; the wind made me colder. The only pedaling I did was to keep my legs moving as the bike and I, pulled by gravity, fell down the mountain. I have exceeded 40 miles per hour on some mountain roads, but speeding down now I had to squeeze the brakes occasionally just to stay under 30 miles per hour! This road was wet, as well as steep, and I didn't want to skid. I was glad I had kept the rear caution light blinking because of the clouds and fog and flat light; I couldn't stop to turn it on now.

By the time I reached Cooper Heights, I had rolled out from under the fog, and the grade was less steep. It was almost sunny, and definitely warmer. At the junction inside the SOCO store, I found a small deli, serving barbecue on a large roll. I ate one, hungrily, with coffee. The two women working there advised me not to take GA 136. It went over the mountain and was quite hilly. A young man said he drove to school through Dahlonega and never went on GA 136 because it had such steep hills, he had to put his pickup in first gear. That convinced me.

They suggested I proceed north on 193, alongside the railroad through the valley. Then I could take 2 and 41 to 52, and follow 52 across the mountains. It would be a hilly ride, but not as steep as 136. The suggestion would keep me closer to the perimeter of Georgia, but would not include New Echota or Dahlonega, where the first gold rush in the United States occurred. I'd miss the gold museum, too. They convinced me the route would get me to Ringgold tonight. I looked at the map and thought, if I could get to Ringgold, or 10 to 20 miles beyond to Dalton, I'd be able to get home from there in one or two days. Shortly before 3:00 P.M., I headed north on 193. The road bore out all their advice. It was a great choice; the ride was warm and pleasant. The clouds lifted, and by the time I reached the far end of the valley, I could look up and see the ridge of Lookout Mountain in Tennessee.

A hawk sitting on a wire between the road and the railroad took off as I came by and flew slightly above the wires beside me for about a quarter-mile. It was brown, about the size of a crow, with brown and white bars on its tail and a whitish breast. The rolly-polly road continued along the railroad, significant in the Battle of Chicamauga. A sign advertised "Baby Chicks, brown egg layers, $1 each." I rode through the Chickamauga Valley, passing a sign for "Old Chickamauga Valley Road," which led to the other side of the railroad and the site of the battlefield. Last year I'd spent time there during a bicycle ride tracing Sherman's march across Georgia.

I passed through Flintstone, Georgia — not on my map — and continued north. After pedaling 52 miles, I turned right on GA 2 and headed through Fort Oglethorpe toward Ringgold. I rolled over Chickamauga Creek several times, then entered Ringgold. I had rounded the northeast corner of Georgia's perimeter; I was headed home!

A bicyclist caught up with me on a rattly, clunky bike and asked if I'd like to go to Waffle House for water. I was thirsty, and my bottles were empty. He said his name was T.J., and that he had worked there but didn't have a job now. He wanted to be a bicycle racer, but was having trouble getting sponsors. He didn't look to me like any of the racers I knew, and his bicycle was a severe handicap. We went in and drank water, and he went to talk with some of the workers. I left, but he followed me out the door. "I'll ride along and keep you company."

"Thanks, I have to stop and make some phone calls first."

"Are you staying here?"

"I don't know yet, I have to ask some questions, and see what develops during the calls. I enjoyed talking with you. Goodbye."

He got on his bike. I rolled mine next door to the Econolodge, where I secured a room. It was only about 5:00 P.M., and I hadn't been feeling tired but now I had no will to pedal further. Another 15 miles to Dalton had seemed a great idea, until I stopped. Three glasses of water and pleading fatigue to T.J. convinced me I could go no further. I didn't want to make the effort which conversation required, in addition to riding this late in the day.

The moment I flipped on the TV, and saw that the golf game was just ending, I was thankful to T. J. I had been so tired, I'd forgotten my intention of halting early and staying in a motel to watch the golf match.

Assisted by several glasses of water, and the end of my bag of popcorn, I settled down to root for Tom Watson. He didn't pull off the win.

Before going to sleep, I walked across the street for some spaghetti at Pizza Hut.

Ringgold, Monday, April 15

A pancake breakfast is one of the few meals that I will eat at McDonald's. Omitting the butter and meat, I slathered the cakes with syrup (although sometimes I leave that off too), and drank orange juice and decaffeinated coffee. Heading east on US 76 after breakfast, I stopped at the Ringgold courthouse to photograph the depot and the eternal flame to veterans of all wars. During the Battle of Ringgold Gap in 1863, Confederates around the old depot managed to hold the gap from Union control long enough for the main army to establish a defense line around Dalton.

Traveling US 76 made me think of my Rabun County house, which is only two miles off that highway. Every time I passed a US shield with a 76 on it, I pedaled with greater urgency. When a truckload of live chickens passed by, a few feathers swirled at me, and the pungent fragrance of chicken swirled with them. US 76 then took me past Tunnel Hill, another important Civil War landmark, and through Dalton.

Dalton claims over 200 carpet mills and almost as many outlet stores, the Carpet Capital of the World. As a former rug merchant, it amused me to pedal through this area because so many enterprises have something to do with the rug industry or its support. I had dealt with handmade, one-of-a-kind Tibetan rugs, on quite a small scale, although for a short time I probably had the largest new Tibetan rug selection in America. I wondered about Dalton's "capital-of-the-world" claim — maybe for machine-made carpets. My interest had been new rugs that repeated historic designs. People who value quality enough to pay for it wanted old rugs, which were rare. After eight years, I replaced my interest in rugs with bicycling.

Red clover was in bloom along the road — vast carpets of it — top-quality artistry, certified by nature.

I was getting a headache, and attributed it to the coffee I had drunk the day before. I was eating less, though, so it might have indicated hunger. A truckload of newly made pallets, similar to those I saw in a lumberyard the day before, went by smelling of fresh cut wood. It was clear enough to see the silhouette of the mountains, but not sunny enough for sunglasses. The overcast days were welcome; I had too much sunburn on my legs. As long as I pedaled to keep the bicycle going, 65 degrees was comfortable wearing a T-shirt.

Although four lanes wide, the road's paved shoulder provided a safe place to ride. Best of all, it was graded for trucks going through the mountains, which made it easier for me, too. After yesterday's quiet among pine trees and clouds, it was almost refreshing to be on a busy highway.

At Chatsworth, I turned east on GA 52 and got as far as Cantrell's grocery when hunger struck. I ate a made-from-scratch hamburger, with lettuce, tomato, onion, and mustard, and washed it down with V8 juice. A banana and popcorn were dessert. Rested and ready to go, I wondered about the road, and asked a man in the store. He didn't know. Another man overheard my question and suggested that I get off GA 52, because it is very steep and goes over the mountain. By taking Old Federal Road, "Over there," he pointed, I could go around the mountain and stay in the valley. While hilly, it wouldn't be as steep. He explained turns that would put me out on US 76 again, headed for Ellijay. I took his advice, followed his instructions carefully, and had a fine ride. The narrow valleys along Dennis Mill Road, with farms in the bottomlands and a few cattle here and there, reminded me of the steep, narrow Rabun County terrain. After about 40 miles since morning, I came to a tough seven-mile climb that took a long time. I was proceeding at the grand pace of 2.5 miles per hour. But it gave me the chance to look more closely at the butterflies and the trees. Changes in the wind told me when I reached intermediate passes or a small ridge. I even found tadpoles in a puddle. Like most children, I had enjoyed playing with tadpoles, watching the hind frog legs develop and studying the tiny frogs.

I kept rolling over the letters "RWM" painted on the road, with an arrow pointing to the right. At first, I looked in the ditch, then thought to look a little further and confirmed that they indicated the presence of a cement right-of-way marker.

By 2:00 P.M., I was exhausted and had been out of water for a while. I began to descend at last, and stopped at PawPaws Grocery for a decaffeinated Diet Coke and a bag of Tom's Peanuts. The grocery was brand new, not even fully stocked yet. The owner complained that the delivery people had not come. He was struggling to install a screen door, but he stopped to fill one of my water bottles, and I sat on the front steps, sipping water, chewing on peanuts, and talking with him about how to fix the door. He had built the store with windows only on the front, so with no cross ventilation it was hot inside. He said the drink freezers and a bait bubbler created more inside heat than he'd expected. He hoped a screen door would correct the problem. Unfortunately, the placement of the lock fixture interfered with its installation. He wouldn't move the lock fixture, because he said the nails were too long and he couldn't get them out. Since I've never built anything, all I had to offer were opinions, but I didn't credit them much. When I left, he was still mumbling about the door. Even with no door, it was hot inside without the "air" turned on. He said it was too early in the spring for that.

I felt much better, and proceeded from the Tails Creek area to Ellijay. The town apparently had a large chicken-processing plant. I noticed a parking lot full of truck-trailers, loaded with empty chicken baskets. It was near a building that looked similar to one I'd seen in Salisbury, Maryland, where chickens are processed. Perhaps the plastic-wrapped chicken parts were loaded into refrigerator trucks on the other side.

On the corner, I ate at a Hardee's and pedaled toward Blue Ridge about 4:00 P.M. The afternoon was fine, and I didn't think another 15 miles would be too tough. Dogwood and redbud were just blooming at this altitude. Soon I passed through Cherry Log and came to a marker noting that the home of Indian Chief Whitepath had stood nearby, from 1800 to 1982.

Continuing along the road shoulder, I was really moving fast down a long grade when a woman in a pickup started a turn across the four-lane road into a side road several hundred yards ahead of me. She hesitated at the median. I thought she had seen me until she pulled across in front of me! By the time she started, I couldn't stop. Apparently, she realized what was going on, but didn't know what to do. She pulled out, almost stopped again dead ahead of me, then stepped on the gas and got out of my way. Her hesitation really scared us both. If she had paused a few instants longer, I would have broadsided her truck or wrecked, trying to miss her. I couldn't go in front, because she might suddenly move; behind her was gravel and a poor surface, so I probably would have developed a skid or fallen. She did move, though, and all was well. I rolled on, and it wasn't until I gasped for air that I realized I'd been holding my breath.

It's hard for vehicle drivers to judge the speed of a bicycle, because most of them are unaccustomed to such encounters. Therefore I think it is the bicyclist's responsibility to make all the right judgments, because most of us have experience as both bicyclists and vehicle operators. For this reason, I have ridden to raise money for the League of American Wheelmen's Education Fund. One of its goals is to see that more and more people, especially school children, are taught bicycling techniques and safety, similar to life-saving and first-aid classes.

Curiously, in our culture, children are given bicycles and admonished NEVER to ride in the "dangerous" street. At least two generations of Americans have grown up believing the streets are dangerous for bicyclists. I do not believe that is true. The streets are not dangerous. It is the lack of consideration and understanding about where to ride bicycles safely, and lack of acceptance of responsibility for control of your vehicle, that impede safety. Fear based on ignorance is a normal response, but it can be overcome with ability and knowledge. Giving in to ignorance and fear was not what built America, and will not strengthen our citizens or our government.

I had planned to continue another four miles, to Lakeview Inn Motel, but when I reached the hilltop on which a Days Inn was perched it was 6:00 P.M. and getting dark. I saw another long, steep climb about a mile and a half ahead, and wondered what the next four miles would require of me. I asked about the senior citizen rate at the Days Inn; it was so reasonable, my decision was made. It was a good thing, as it turned out. The next morning I never saw the Lakeview Inn, and I would have been caught by darkness far from the nearest town. Seventy-five miles through these mountains was quite a satisfactory day's work, of course, but I knew steeper mountains were ahead, and I wasn't sure exactly how far it was to my house. Probably about as far as I'd traveled today, only more difficult. I got a *USA Today* paper and went to my room, determined to rise early and go however far it was to reach home.

There was no real need to keep emergency food, or carry its weight, so supper consisted of the last can of tunafish with rye Triskets, and V8. I'd bought a slimming canned drink, but it tasted so bad I threw it out. I also finished up an odd assortment of snacks, one of which broke a tooth out of my upper denture. I walked to the Texaco station store nearby, in search of Crazy Glue. Luckily, they had it. Fortunately, the glue held the tooth into the top denture. Though the program on the Discovery channel was interesting, it couldn't keep me awake long.

Blue Ridge, Tuesday, April 16

Anxious to be on the road, I awoke at 6:00 A.M. and ate breakfast at Waffle King. I was ready to roll by 7:00 A.M., but it was too foggy. Fifteen minutes later I could see twice as far. I hoped this would be the last day of my perimeter bicycle tour of Georgia. Did I really want it to end, or was I just ready to rest awhile? As with vacations, I couldn't wait to begin the tour; now I would be glad to get home.

I expected to cover about 70 miles, two-thirds of it in hills. About one-third of yesterday's route was hills, with longer mileage. Because it might be the last day, I could probably push enough to get home, but this would be a tough day, regardless. Well, at least it would begin with a long downhill roll. There would be plenty of uphills.

Had I known it would rain so much and be so cold, I would have given the tent and the rest of the cooking things to Sue Smith. I would have kept the sleeping bag for emergencies and because I use it in motels instead of turning on the heat.

About 7:30 A.M., I turned on the rear caution blinker, put my feet into the toe clips, and began to roll downhill. There was almost no traffic. In the first two and a half hours, I covered 20 miles. Then I spent half an hour in the McDonald's at Blairsville, eating three pancakes and drinking orange juice. I read the Atlanta paper and consulted the map. The road appeared to follow a valley, then go over a big mountain just before Hiawassee. Then it had to go down, because I knew there should be an upgrade before US 76 crossed the Appalachian Trail' which followed a ridge.

On the road again, I wished I had followed my own advice. Two pancakes with syrup made me feel terrible. I should have eaten the pancakes without the syrup. Even better, I could have stuck with fruit and juices. But the way I was pushing the pedals, I would soon work it off. I stopped to remove my long pants and wind jacket, and rode the rest of the day in shorts and a cotton T-shirt. For the first time in days and days, I had to put on sunglasses! It was a perfectly grand, sunny, warm day.

Proceeding through the valley, I stopped to read that a side road led south crossing Trackrock Gap two miles away. Soapstone boulders in the gap are covered with tracks, symbols, and patterns, carved in the rocks by primitive man. The Cherokees called the gap something that translates into "where there are tracks." One tradition holds that it was the landing place of the big canoe, transporting survivors of a world-wide flood. The heavens are supposed to thunder when a stranger approaches. Well, I'd have to put it on the "come back" list.

Further along, another marker told me I was passing north of Brasstown Bald. It was the high, rounded peak to my south, with a lookout tower. Also known as Mount Enotah, the highest mountain in Georgia at 4,748 feet, it has a grassy, rather than a timbered, summit. Hence the name "Bald." Its Indian name means "place of fresh green." The first white settlers mistook the Indian name for a similar word meaning brass — Brasstown. A forest service road leads to a picnic area near the summit.

Every town I went through on this trip was decked out in yellow ribbons, welcoming military service people home from the Persian Gulf. Signs in store windows often listed their names. In front of schools and National Guard Halls and courthouses and church yards, and on trees, flag poles, cannons, and signs were yellow ribbons, waving a welcome home.

I passed Young Harris College, founded in 1886. Hiawassee was only seven miles ahead, Clayton, 37 miles. "Keep Going!" I ordered.

In Hiawassee, I stopped in a restaurant to read the paper and eat tomatoes and okra, baked beans, and cold slaw. I could have done without the cherry cobbler, but I ate it anyway. I'd never been to Hiawassee, and I was interested in the way the town wanders the lake shores, in an alpine bowl. The air was magnificent, and lakes spread themselves everywhere among fields of cultivated blueberry bushes.

I expect I pedaled above 2,000 feet most of the day. Crawling up the mountain, one revolution of the pedals at a time, finally brought me to the Appalachian Trail. I recognized it by the blue blazes. A man carrying a backpack was about to disappear into the woods. I yelled. He stopped as I pedaled slowly up. Tom Carnein, a through hiker from Connecticut, had walked about a week and expected to finish his trip in five months. He is a heavy fellow and I couldn't help thinking that if he succeeded, he'd emerge at the other end of the trail with a much healthier, thinner body, and a sense of accomplishment that will influence the rest of his life. I envied him a bit, knowing that even if I wanted to hike the trail, I wouldn't be able to do it on my ancient feet. I gave him my apple, orange, and a PowerBar, and wished him well. Unlike a bicyclist, the Appalachian Trail through hiker must be thoroughly organized about supplies, or leave the trail to get food.

Once, in Virginia, I met a through hiker who carried his skate board down from Maine. When I saw him, he was riding it down to the valley to get supplies. He would carry it back up again. Wheels are great for going down!

Just beyond the trail crossing, 48.2 miles from the morning's start, I entered Rabun County. I flew on wings of exuberance — and gravity — downhill for about a mile. Then going up it got so steep, I had to walk a few hundred yards. Last night my knees were a bit sore — tender muscles really — and now, for the first time on this tour, I could feel them while riding. At the top of the rise, no cars came from behind, so I let the bike have its head, guiding it down the switchback road at about 35 miles per hour. After climbing up again, I came to a roadside park and lay on top of a picnic table in the sun, tired of spinning in bottom gear (28/32). I ate a Meal-to-Go bar, drank some water, watched the sun flicker among leaves stirred by the wind blowing up the gap, and marveled at the dogwood I had seen in bloom all along my nearly two-month tour.

I got on the bike again, and soon reached the next pass. I rolled down and down to Lake Burton. At the Tallulah-Persimmon Volunteer Fire Department, I turned left, off US 76 and onto County Route 216. I was headed for home, along a familiar training route, through Persimmon Valley via Germany Road. I knew a two-mile climb awaited me, but so did fresh water near the top. I took the short cut along a rushing trout stream, with May apples in bloom on its banks. Then the climb began, shaded by trees, and cool and damp from streams that cut among mountain laurel bushes and rushed by moss-covered rocks.

Slowly, I struggled upward. I came to the place where on a training ride, I had foolishly gone too fast and fallen, three miles from home. No serious injury, but I was bruised and shaken, and the bicycle chain broke. I had to fix it before I could get home. Since that close call, I carry identification (itemized for the area where I am riding), wear my helmet, and keep my bike under control on mountain curves. As I passed the spot, I was thankful to have had no further mishap since then.

I cranked slowly by a trillium, but it wasn't in bloom yet. At the water pipe, I drank a whole bottle of the cool spring water, knowing the worst climb was nearly over. Only three short, fairly easy hills separated me and home.

When I rode over the last hill, I let the bike fly down Germany Road until I had to brake hard to enter the gravel road to my house. I kept right on going, bumping over the gravel faster than I had ever gone before, knowing that if I had a flat tire now it wouldn't matter. I leaned the loaded bike against the house, and put my key in the front-door lock. I was home!

I found myself thinking of all the places I didn't get to; there's so much more to see in Georgia. What I did was view the state like a live map for 1,587 miles. I met a few people, and compiled a longer list of places to visit than I had when I began. But now, my legs were tired and I would gladly hang up my vagabond habits for awhile — at least until my next adventure.

—— Lesson Plans ——
Dr. Katherine S. Hawes, Memphis State University

Introduction

This book, *Crackers & Peaches*, on bicycling the perimeter
of Georgia with the accompanying study guide printed in the appendix
can be used wth a variety of groups of readers. It allows a holistic approach
to increasing literacy and may be used in the classroom to teach a variety
of subjects including reading and composition as well as science and
social studies. It also allows students to delve into specific areas of
special interest.

Another example of the use of the book is to improve the literacy of
adults. Mrs. Bush and the Literacy Council have increased the emphasis
on improving adult reading beyond the third and fourth grade level.
Current materials focus on jobs and selfl-improvement. Pleasure reading
encourages adults to explore the world beyond their own experience and
learn to treasure reading for the joy and vision it gives them. The book
and the chapter discussion items could be used with these literacy
groups. With adults I would encourage the use of the general items in

small discussion groups where they feel comfortable sharing their own experiences and relating their ideas to your the authors ideas. This book is also suitable for church, community, and prison populations of adult readers.

Local book clubs are literacy groups which are too often overlooked, and yet they are a very popular aspect of American culture. The book would be quite popular, especially in the pring, when readers are looking for an escape from the winterdoldrums and for ideas for summer recreation. The study guide and items for discussion could provide focus and incentive, especially in the early stages of a discussion.

Lesson Plans

Syllabus: Goal (skill, content), objectives, materials, lesson, activity, evaluation, extension activities.

Levels: Grades 6, 7, 8, 9. Emphasis on adventure, heroes, and biographies. (Designed for but not limited to these levels.)

Goals: 1. *Reading skills:* drawing conclusions, reaching main ideas, locating information.
2. *Composition skills:* journal format, sensory impressions.
3. *Content:* geography, science, history of Georgia.
4. *Vocabulary:* biker glossary, geography terms, math and science terms, history terms.
5. *Mapping skills.*
6. *Critical thinking skills:* values, goals, problem solving, criticism, making predictions
7. *Biking skills and safety.*

Materials: book, pen, paper, maps.

Bicycling Glossary: fishtail
panniers
bungee
BRAG
LAW
RAAM   etc....

Contents: Rationale
Collaborative Learning
Introducing the Unit
Daily Procedures
Evaluation
Projects
Extension Activities

Rationale: *Crackers & Peaches* motivates students
to read. This book intrigues the reader with a diary
format which shares the roadside experiences of a keen
observer of Georgia and Georgians. The reader learns
about topics such as native birds, flowers, geography,
economy, foods, and history as prompted by events
along the way. One also learns occassional sugges
tions for biking.

The book is an excellent source for classroom
activities to teach skills as well as content. Students
enjoy drawing the route on a map as they read.
Some may take notes on birds while others note
local economies or write an opinion composition on
social customs. Since the format is a daily diary, it is
easy to assign short reading selections by dates or
longer ones by geographical chapters.

*The following class strategies emphasize collaborative learning in
which everybody does a first reading for general understanding followed by a skimming and scanning for specific details of a project such
as charting birds in each geographical region. Students conclude by
sharing their project information. The time alloted for the study of the
book may be varied according to the degree of specificity desired by the
teacher.*

Directions for Collaborative Activities: Collaboration to solve a problem or complete a task can enhance and enrich the understanding and skills of the student. The activities which accompany this book encourage small-group reading and responding with each person sharing information and ideas before com posing a personal written response. The following suggestions guide group management.

1. Each group should contain about three students.

2. Make three index cards for each topic for the day's lesson. Give one card to each student. This helps assure responses for all acitivities.
   a. Each student silently reads to respond to the direction on the index card.
   b. Students with identical cards discuss their re sponses and complete a written response. The students should write the direction of the index card at the top of the notebook paper followed by the final response for a personal grade.

3. Students researching information for the class wall chart then write the responses on this chart.

4. The teacher may evaluate each paper with a letter/ number grade and total the group's score. The best team receives recognition.

Notes for the Student: Notice that reading activities may ask for general ideas or for specific details. When you read for general ideas, read rapidly as you think about the direction on the index card. After you read, think about your reactions and your own personal ideas. Discuss and share ideas with your group; debate the issue. Then compose your own paragraph. Reading for specific details is a different kind of reading. It is like skimming first lines and scanning for items scattered throughout the chap ter. Skim and scan for items required to locate the information or list of things you need to know. Good study-reading includes both a first reading for general ideas and a second reading for specific details.

Collaborative group behavior expects every member of the group to participate to the best of their ability, to ask another member of the group for help when needed, and to help any partner in trouble so everyone experiences success. Groups may compete with other groups but must work as a team within their own group.

Introducing the Unit: Survey a wall map of Georgia with the class. Ask individual students to point to places they have been and tell what they saw there. Ask them what they liked best. Ask them how they traveled(car, train, bus, etc.). Introduce the book as a journal of a woman who biked around the perimeter of the state, recorded impressions on a tape and with a camera, and typed her notes into a computer daily as she traveled.

Individual Lesson Format: Each day the lesson follows a similar format which may be varied in content and in length as time and interest allow. First, the class should focus on the topic by recalling some of the more interesting events of the journal read the preceding class day. Second, collaborative learning behaviors should be briefly reviewed. Third, group activities should be introduced so that students may consider which topic to choose. Fourth, group activities should be started.

1. Remind the class to mark the route on their personal maps of Georgia.

2. Each student chooses a general purpose from the list and reads to respond. Use index cards to facilitate dispersion of topics and grouping of students.

3. Each group meets and discusses their pre-reading purposes, makes notes, and writes personal responses.

4. Each student chooses a specific purpose from the list and reads to respond. Use index cards to facilitate dispersion of topics and grouping of students.

5. Each group meets and collaborates on the re sponse. Then individuals write their own papers.

Evaluation: Exams on content of the book may include a paragraph essay, vocabulary, and a quiz on specific details. Sug gested paragraph essay topics include the following:

1. Support the following thesis: Georgia is a "State of Adventure." Cite proof.

2. Support the following thesis: Georgia is a "Land of Opportunity." Cite proof.

Projects and Games Discussion of class lessons at home is encouraged by projects which are assigned at school to be completed at home. The following activities are usually popular:

1. Make a map of Jane's route through Georgia.

2. Make a collage poster titled "Georgia on My Mind."

3. Make complete plans for a simulated Georgia bike tour including route, dates, clothing, food, over night plans, contingency plans, etc.

Games and contests help reinforce memory of details and vocabulary discussed in class. The following games are often successful without too much class disruption:

1. Scandalous Scanning: Two teams compete in speed in locating details named by the teacher or game leader. Give a point to the team which first locates the item in the book. The first team to reach twenty one points is the winner.

2. Two to five teams compete to see which team can follow Jane's route and get back to Clayton first. Team scores from daily collaborative activities may be mul tiplied by a common factor and plotted as miles on Jane's route.

3. Vocabulary Jigsaw: Give a list of bikers' terms or other types of vocabulary to each team captain. The list should be divided into clusters of five words. Team members split the list and regroup with other team members who have the same portion of the list. They discuss their words, clarify their meanings, and write a definition for each one. Then team members return to their original team to teach each other with discussion and flash card drills. After the class takes the vocabu lary test, the teacher figures the team total score and recognizes the team with the highest score.

Daily Chapter Activity Lists

Chapter One: Running Downhill _____

Suggestions for a general first reading:(Choose one.)

1. Read the chapter to see if you think you would enjoy such a bike trip. List the things you like; then list the things you don't like.

2. Read the chapter to see what aspect of her trip Jane likes best. Give several examples to explain why she does.

3. Describe Jane based on what she does, what she says, and how other people respond to her. Do you think you would like her? Why?

Suggestions for a specific second reading:(Choose one.)

1. Name the birds she sees.

2. Name the jobs of the people she meets.

3. Describe the land elevations.

4. Explain how she packed for a bike trip.

5. Start a glossary of bicycling terms, definitions, and drawings.

6. Start a list of plant life she sees.

7. What determines how far a biker can travel in a day?

8. List the people Jane meets.

9. Start a time line(1600 - 1950; 25 years equals one-half inch) and note items dated by Jane such as explorers, settlers, and Native Americans.

Chapter Two: Coasting _____

Suggestions for a general first reading:(Choose one.)

1. Read the chapter to see how the Atlantic Ocean affects Georgians. List these effects.

2. Read the chapter and explain why you would or would not like to live in this area. State your opinion and list three to five reasons why.

3. Read the chapter to see if Jane learned much about Georgia history in this area. Explain your conclusion.

4. Read in order to determine if Jane liked this area. List three reasons as proof of your decision.

Suggestions for a specific second reading:(Choose one.)

1. Continue the activity you started for chapter one.

2. Choose another activity listed for chapter one.

3. Read in order to write an imaginary dialogue Jane might have with a native resident of that area.

4. Read in order to list the three most interesting bits of information described about this area.

5. Read in order to list the foods Jane ate while in this area.

6. Read in order to list the foods Jane eats when she eats in her tent.

Chapter Three: Westward _____

Suggestions for a general first reading:(Choose one.)

1. Read the chapter to determine the effect of westerly winds on a biker. List the good and bad effects.

2. Read the chapter to find out what Jane learned about the water system in this geographical area. Does she think this is important? Why?

3. Read the chapter to learn how the weather had changed since she left Clayton. Describe the weather at this point of the trip.

Suggestions for a specific second reading:(Choose one.)

1. Continue an activity started in a preceding chapter.

2. Start a new activity listed in a preceding chapter.

3. Make a skeletal outline of the chapter.

4. Make a time line for Jane's events in this chapter.

5. Write the dialogue for a radio interview with Jane about her impres

sions of the swamps.

6. When Jane turned north, did her route become an uphill one? List reasons why.

7. What impressed Jane about Thomasville? List items.

Chapter Four: Upstream _____

Suggestions for a general first reading:(Choose one.)

1. Read to find out how dependability was important on Jane's trip.

2. Read to determine why you think Jane became so tired at Seminole Camp Ground.

3. Read to learn about Jane's opinion of social values.

4. Read to analyze how sensory impressions affect the journalistic style of writing.

5. Read to learn the complexities of historical restoration.

6. Read to determine why "grass roots" politics is so strong in the "Upstream" area.

Suggestions for a specific second reading:(Choose one.)

1. Continue a preceding activity.

2. Choose another activity from a preceding chapter list.

3. Read in order to list what pleasures you share with Jane.

4. Read in order to list problems bikers have with camping.

5. Read in order to list the forms of communication critiqued by Jane.

6. Read in order to list the forms of architecture observed by Jane.

7. Read in order to list the effects of weather on Jane and on other people she encountered.

8. Draw a time line for the history of the "Upstream" area.

9. Read in order to list the effects of rivers and oceans on communities.

Chapter Five: Hometown _____

Suggestions for a general first reading:(Choose one.)

1. Read to determine Jane's emotions about her "homecoming."

2. Read to understand collaboration as Jane perceived it.

Suggestions for a specific second reading:(Choose one.)

1. Continue an activity from the preceding chapter.

2. Choose another activity from a preceding chapter.

3. Read to list pointers in planting pine trees.

4. Read to list steps to follow to be in bike time trials.

5. Read to list Jane's family and their influence on her wide range of interests.

Suggestions for a general first reading:(Choose one.)

1. Read to learn how a bike tour can help a person learn to cope with fear.

2. Read to determine how weather affected Jane emotionally.

3. Read to learn how biking in north Georgia is different compared to biking in southwest Georgia.

Suggestions for a specific second reading:(Choose one.)

1. Continue an activity from the preceding chapter.

2. Choose another activity from a preceding chapter.

3. Read to list the problems of bicycling groups.

4. Read to draw a picture of bike chains and gears.

5. Read to list safety tips for bikers on north Georgia highways.

Extensions: Extension activities can carry students beyond the class lessons and activities and lead them to explore topics and skills in greater depth. The following activities should be considered:

Activities: 1. Start an anecdotal journal like Jane's.

2. Interview a person or people in your neighbor hood about why they live in Georgia, their job, their ancestors. Use a tape recorder. Write an

interesting article to share your interview with other class members.

3. Read an article in a bicycling magazine.

4. Make a booklet on observations of birds in your community.

5. Make a booklet on observations of flowers and/or trees in your community.

6. Plan a bike trip telling where, when, what to take, how much money, food, camping gear, etc.

7. Read a biography of one of the historical people mentioned in the book.

8. Write an opinion paper on the social customs of people visiting in campgrounds.

9. Research your favorite stop on Jane's trip.

edited by Georgina M. Mundell

The Bicycle Ride Across Georgia is known by its initials as BRAG.

BRAG is a family-oriented annual bicycle tour. It is not a race. It is recreational, social, and in many ways educational. While it is a strenuous journey of six days, it is completed regularly by anyone from ages six to eighties. On the ride you'll meet students, pilots, judges, soldiers, teachers, and retirees, alone or in groups of friends or families. The journey is made easy or difficult by the rider's training in advance and pedaling speed and other efforts during the tour.

The annual BRAG route changes so that you can see Georgia at the quiet, unhurried pace of a bicycle ride. You'll discover things about Georgia, and about yourself, that you never expected.

Each year the trip takes cyclists over the lightly traveled back roads, through small towns and rural countryside. Riders leave each morning whenever they like and travel the route at their own pace. They meet at the end of the day and set up camp. Since camping's not for everyone, some riders choose to stay at local motels. Entertainment or activities are available in the evening. The townspeople go out of their way to ensure that his or her BRAG bicyclists have a great time.

During the week everyone is responsible for their own meals. Where there are few restaurants, local churches and civic groups provide them at reasonable prices.

BRAG is organized in mid-June. Current information may be obtained from any bicycle club in Georgia. Some of them are listed below:

Augusta Free Wheelers
113 Mistywoods Dr.
Grovetown, GA 30813

Bicycle Assn. of North Georgia: B.A.N.G.
RR 7 Box 174A
Canton, GA 30114-9807

Chicken City Cyclists
3534 Westgate Dr.
Gainesville, GA 30504

Coastal Bicycle Touring Club
1326 Grace Dr.
Savannah, GA 31406-6917

Coosa Valley Cycling Assn.
P.O. Box 2764
Rome, GA 30164-2764

Emerald City Bicycle Club
1812 Knox Street
Dublin, GA 31021-5519

Gwinnett Touring Club
P.O. Box 464365
Lawrenceville, GA 30246

Middle Georgia Bicycle Club
P.O. Box 2083
Macon, GA 31203-2083

Pecan City Pedalers, Inc.
P.O.Box 214
Albany, GA 31702-0214

Southern Bicycle League
P.O. Box 1360
Roswell, GA 30077

Southern Cyclists
P.O. Box 2554
Statesboro, GA 30458-9998

The list on the previous page is printed with thanks to the League of American Wheelmen (L.A.W.). It comes from their annual *Bicycle USA Almanac* ($8.00) available from:

L.A.W.
190 W. Ostend Street, Suite 120
Baltimore, MD 21230-3755
voice (410) 539-3399, fax (410) 539-3496

The almanac lists similar and additional information for every state. Each year it lists major bicycling events in each state together with how to obtain more information. L.A.W's magazine for members is full of information, articles, and color photographs. One of the questions I hear most is, "Where can I ride my bicycle?" These L.A.W. publications answer on a national scale.

For more information, ask for books and guides in your local bicycle shop or library. There is much information available, so ask for it to get current data beyond the scope of this book.

Milner Press

office: 3842 Windom Pl NW, Washington, DC 20016
sales: 715 Miami Circle NE, Atlanta, GA 30024, 404-231-9107

(next book due for publication in fall 1993)
To order send check payable to Milner Press to either adress.

Changing Gears
Bicycling America's Perimeter
$22 postpaid

OR

Crackers & Peaches
Travels in Georgia
$12 postpaid

Thanks to Barbara Daniel for arranging that Georgia maps be included in each copy of this book and to Karin Pendley Koser for the cover comment. For more information about Georgia contact a visitors center or:

Georgia Department of Industry, Trade and Tourism
285 Peachtree Center Avenue, NE
P.O. Box 1776
Atlanta, GA 30301-1776
fax: (404) 656-3567